Bicycling Magazine's
Long-Distance Cycling

By the Editors of *Bicycling* Magazine

 Rodale Press, Emmaus, Pennsylvania

Our Mission

We publish books that empower people's lives.

RODALE BOOKS

If you have any questions or comments concerning this book, please write:
    Rodale Press
    Book Readers' Service
    33 East Minor Street
    Emmaus, PA 18098

Library of Congress Cataloging-in-Publication Data

Bicycling magazine's long-distance cycling / by the editors of Bicycling magazine.
        p.   cm.
    ISBN 0–87596–155–X paperback
    1. Cycling—Training.   I. Bicycling magazine Apr. 1987–
GV1048.B49   1993
796.6—dc20   92-33508
                                          CIP

Distributed in the book trade by St. Martin's Press

2 4 6 8 10 9 7 5 3 1 paperback

Long-Distance Cycling

CONTENTS

◼ INTRODUCTION

No matter what distance you aspire to, this book provides the expert advice to help you ride longer and stronger than ever before. We've selected the newest and best information on endurance cycling published in *Bicycling* magazine. It's short on theory and long on practicality—the same techniques used by the best long-distance riders to improve their stamina, strength, comfort, nutrition and bike-handling skills.

This is the kind of book that every long-distance riding enthusiast wishes he or she had to show the way. Now you can learn in hours what it has taken many endurance cyclists years of trial and error to discover. Although the ability to ride great distances isn't developed overnight, the skill will come as quickly as possible if you heed the advice within. First we emphasize how to ride the first or best century of your life, then we give you the know-how to go beyond.

Good luck! See you on the road. . . .

The editors of *Bicycling* magazine

Part One

CHALLENGES
TO ENDURANCE

PARIS-BREST-PARIS: THE KING OF LONG-DISTANCE EVENTS

Every four years, riders from around the world gather in Paris, France, to renew an event nearly as old as cycling itself. This endurance challenge, known simply as Paris-Brest-Paris, or PBP, takes them west through the undulating French farm country to the seacoast town of Brest, then back to the starting point. The distance is 760 miles, but as if this weren't tough enough, a strict time limit is imposed. To be an official finisher, the cyclist must complete the ride in 90 hours or less. This puts a premium not only on physical fitness but also on the dogged determination to keep pedaling through any weather and with minimal sleep.

For many, Paris-Brest-Paris defines what it is to be a long-distance cyclist. As explained at the end of this chapter, participation is gained through a yearlong series of qualifying rides, known as brevets. In 1991, more than 3,200 cyclists from two dozen countries earned the right to ride in PBP's centennial event. Included were 398 Americans, and among them was Bicycling *editor Ed Pavelka. Here is his story.*

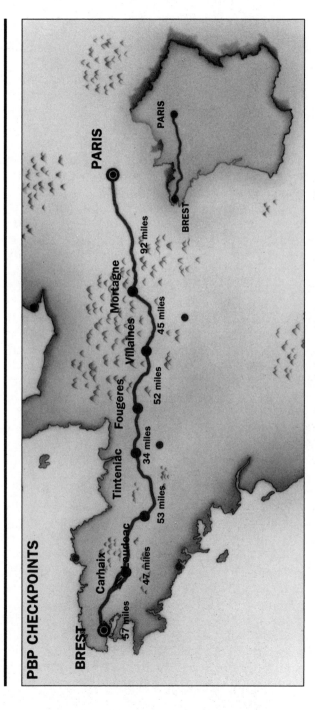

PBP CHECKPOINTS

PARIS

92 miles

Mortagne

Villaines
45 miles

Fougeres
52 miles

Tinteniac
34 miles

Loudeac
53 miles

Carhaix
47 miles

BREST
57 miles

PARIS

BREST

A rider who completes the 380 miles from Paris to Brest is only halfway in the quest to complete the famous PBP endurance event.

I watched from the corner of my eye as she read the account of a Paris-Brest-Paris waged long ago. It told a tale of fatigue, misery and mechanical breakdown during wind-swept days and long, cold, sleepless nights. It described zombielike riders pushing uncertainly through 1,200 kilo-meters of ceaseless French hills, unable to steer a straight line or even recognize the other riders around them.

Slowly she moved forward in her chair until, sitting bolt upright, she turned toward me and exclaimed, "This is torture! I suppose you're going to torture yourself."

"No way, Ma," I replied with a cool confidence partly calculated to soothe a parent's fear. "That's why I'm doing all this training. It won't be torture for me."

Okay, so why am I strapped to this gurney, being wheeled by French medics through a maze of hallways to an emergency room? How come the white tile ceiling is be-ginning to spin and I'm seconds from flooding the place with the liter of Evian water I just drank?

"Hot! Hot! Hot!" I yell, struggling to free my arms and tear off my sweat-soaked jersey. Don't they understand? Cool me down, please—and bring a bucket before I. . .

Too late. The chair next to the gurney gets soaked by four gushing eruptions, and I roll onto my back feeling the momentary relief that comes with finally getting it over with. In a scene from a nightmare, those around me are laughing and jabbering words I can't understand. I turn my head to see a bewildered nurse, who had arrived seconds late and with a ridiculously small pan. On reflection, I guess it was kind of funny.

At last, an English-speaking doctor arrives and begins tests to determine exactly what's wrong. Meanwhile, an at-tendant pokes and shakes me each time I close my eyes. I think she's afraid I won't wake up.

"You will be fine," the doctor says after reading the EKG and blood test. "It is heat exhaustion, nothing worse. Rest now and you..."

I don't hear any more as I sink into a deep sleep, my first in a day and a half. I had finished PBP two hours ago, riding into the stadium in Guyancourt, west of Paris, under a piercing sun after dueling a headwind since the turn-around at Brest 380 miles before. I felt good upon arriving—

happy, proud and not just a little emotional. No, PBP wasn't torture. But that extra 14 miles I tried to ride to my hotel, through the traffic fumes and heat of the city, certainly was. I suppose PBP made a few riders sick. It certainly took many to their physical and mental brink. At times the roadside resembled the aftermath of some gentle catastrophe, with dozens of motionless bodies in repose. More than 600 of the 3,281 starters decided not to get up again. They quit; some because they couldn't go on, others because they wouldn't.

And then there's the man who has proven to be above it all, Scott Dickson. In one of those crazy coincidences, he happened to be there when I finished and was the first person to greet me. He'd been back for a day, having successfully defended his 1987 title with a 21-minute victory over fellow American Dennis Hearst. Word of his win had drifted down the course, and I congratulated him for another amazing ride. Getting to Brest and back in 43 hours, 42 minutes (12 minutes off the record) is a feat equal to any in cycling, but this slightly built, soft-spoken, 42-year-old from Iowa City makes it seem easy. In four PBPs dating to 1979, he has finished no worse than third and never been slower than 49 hours. And he completed each ride without a minute of sleep.

Dickson calls the 1991 event the "easiest" he has ridden, but this doesn't discount the difficult headwind or additional climbing, which upped the vertical gain to about 35,000 feet. He refers instead to the driving force in his victory, the tandem piloted by Race Across America (RAAM) veterans Bob Breedlove and Richard Fedrigon. Going for a division record, they charged off the front of the competitive 80-hour group, and just four others went with them: Dickson, Hearst, the Pete Penseyres/Jon Royer tandem and a Frenchman intent only on being first to Brest, then getting into his car. And that's what he did, seizing the opportunity when Dickson touched a rear wheel and fell on the outskirts of the seacoast town. As the Frenchman fled, the Americans waited for Dickson to dust himself off and check for damage.

As Penseyres/Royer fell off the pace, Breedlove/Fedrigon kept their big gears turning and the chasers at bay. In fact, they were going so fast that some official checkpoints had yet to open. Enjoying this 19-hour sleigh ride to Brest, Dickson and Hearst were still relatively fresh after the turn-around when the tandem began lagging on climbs. When it also suffered a flat and word arrived that a small group of French chasers was within 20 minutes, it was time to go on without the big bike. The American pair was never caught, but Dickson chose to pull for the entire 34 miles between the checkpoints at Tinteniac and Fougeres to ensure victory.

Swearing he wouldn't try to win after Dickson did so much to buttress their lead, Hearst nevertheless closed several gaps during the last 3 hours. This worried Dickson, who decided to pour it on the next time he gained some distance, which was happening on climbs as Hearst couldn't quite handle the champion's pace. "It was time to find out what he was made of," said Dickson of his decision to drop onto his aero bar and time trial to the finish. When this happened, Hearst, a four-time PBP participant and second American finisher in 1983, never regained contact. Still, he rode strongly to preserve second place, some 2½ hours ahead of the Frenchmen Herve Talabardon and François Thoraval. Breedlove/Fedrigon arrived in 48:07, good for fifth place overall and the tandem record.

Dickson rode a Trek 2300 fitted with Shimano Dura-Ace components and Grip Shift. The 7-speed gearing featured 53/40-tooth chainrings and a 12/18T cogset. Bladed spokes and the bolt-on bar were his only aero equipment. Nutritionally, he relied on Exceed energy bars and drinks, as well as sandwiches, fruit, soup and even a chocolate croissant. Past PBPs had taught him the importance of keeping blood sugar levels high to prevent depression and hallucinations. He abstains from caffeine for several months before each PBP, thus receiving the maximum boost when he uses it in the final 12 hours.

But more than anything, Dickson banks on intelligence and training to ensure success. He says each PBP provides insight for improving equipment and tactics, making victory more a matter of experience than strength. Still, he's supremely fit. His annual mileage has been in the 20,000 to 24,000 range for years, and he trained 16,000 miles during the eight months from January to PBP. He emphasizes speed as well as distance, riding hard most afternoons with local racers after doing solo miles at daybreak. In addition, he competes in races and competitive distance events as often as possible. The Register's Annual Great Bicycle Ride Across Iowa (RAGBRAI) is an annual high point, serving as an informal seven-day stage race as he blasts across Iowa in the company of top-category United States Cycling Federation (USCF) riders. In a sense, he approaches PBP the same way, viewing it as a race from control to control rather than one huge effort.

Dickson says he rides PBP because, "It's a lot of fun, although I'm glad it only takes place every four years because it's so difficult to prepare. The main thing I get out of it is a sense of accomplishment. It makes everything else in life look much less formidable."

Winning Women

Nothing seems too much for affable Elaine Mariolle, either. The 1986 RAAM champion rode her first PBP, wedging the event between sightseeing the land of her ancestors and taking a 600-mile bike tour through Switzerland. "I just thought I'd like to be part of PBP's 100th anniversary celebration," she declared upon arriving at Paris's Orly Airport. "It's a neat tradition."

When the gun sounded, Mariolle's competitive instincts took over. A member of the fast 80-hour group, she powered her custom Eistentraut with the lead men and left all other women behind. Soon she became the princess of the pack, never having to take a pull or bridge a gap alone, thanks to Gallic chivalry (if not chauvinism). "I got adopted by a lot of riders," she explained. "They would motion for me to sit in. I was treated very well."

With this help, Mariolle, rolling on tires pumped to 140 psi, went for the victory and allowed herself only 15 minutes of sleep. "I rode it like a road race," she said. "My goal was to ride well enough and strong enough to win. It turned out to be one of the best experiences I ever had on a bike. One of the hardest experiences, too."

Along the way, shifter trouble kept her from using the big chainring, limiting her high gear to 39 × 14T for a couple hundred miles. During the second night, she had "bizarre" perceptions of riders coming toward her when all she could see were their lights and reflectors. And then, between the final checkpoint and the finish, she got lost and took six hours to ride the remaining 28 miles.

Nevertheless, her time of 62:11 was the best among the 80-hour women, and she received a winner's accolades. Hours later, however, it became known that another woman, Nicole Chabirand of France, was riding strongly in one of the two groups that started later. When this 45-year-old mother of two finished in 59:43, Mariolle's elation turned to disappointment, but she wouldn't allow herself to be down for long. "I did my best," she said a day later, "and it was neat to come in first in my group. After all, PBP is really about doing as well as you can and completing it. It's not just riding a bike, it's people, geography and history. If you want to let up on your pedals to enjoy a field of sunflowers or the sunset, it would be a shame not to because you're tied to the clock. If you want a better sense of what France is about and that means going a little slower, so be it.

"It still wasn't that slow," the 34-year-old added with her trademark chuckle. "I don't think I gathered too much moss out there."

A Cat-and-Mouse Game on Wheels

Nor did I, although as I study my ride it's shocking how much time is lost by riding unsupported. Dozens of cyclists, including Dickson, Hearst, Chabirand and Mariolle, were able to dash through checkpoints because they had someone outside to provide food, drink, clothes—even massage and bike repairs. Meanwhile, most of us in the pack did it the old-fashioned way, carrying everything we would need, plus money to buy additional calories at checkpoints or stores along the course. We never went hungry, but we also took time out to eat and so forth. In my case, each of the dozen stops (not counting Brest, where I spent four hours to wash, sleep and eat a meal) took an average of 45 minutes. Probably the most widespread comment heard after the event was, "Next time I'm going to have support."

Next time? Following the obligatory, "How'd you do?" the postmortem exam always included, "You coming back in '95?" For many the answer changed from "no way" to "we'll see" as sleep and nourishment began tilting the balance between hardship and accomplishment. For every rider who announced plans to sell his lights and fenders and scale back to one-day rides, two others were discussing what they'd do to improve their performance four years hence.

The majority finished in the final half day, their primary goal being to earn the title of "ancien," or one who has completed PBP. As one rider explained, "It's a matter of bonding, of sharing a difficult task with other people. Most of us aren't athletes, but we can endure as long as anyone in the world."

Indeed, many PBP participants, especially the Americans, it seems, aren't athletes by the usual definition. The typical U.S. rider is in his forties and without an impressive background in cycling or any other sport. Compared with a European, he is much less likely to have the well-defined leg muscles, lithe posture, supple pedal stroke and bike-handling skills of an ex–road racer. But he is much more likely to have an aero bar, helmet, rearview mirror and enough gear to ride from Paris to Moscow and back. His bike is generally newer and better, and proof that anything from a Kestrel to a Colnago can be force-fed fenders.

Europeans pace the ride differently, going fast between checkpoints, then enjoying a long meal. Several times I arrived at one in the company of half a dozen 20-mph Frenchmen, only to see them still conversing over food as I departed. Some would also drink wine or beer (one glass for now, one in the bottle for later), and a few were seen smoking at roadside cafes. No, this isn't your usual athletic event.

But maybe they know something I don't, because diet became my major difficulty. I carried Exceed energy bars, replacement fluids and nutritional supplements, using them exclusively and successfully for the first 24 hours. But beginning with breakfast in Brest, I began to also eat regular food at checkpoints every 3 to 4 hours. That's when the trouble started. The pasta, grains, potatoes, bread, pastries, rice pudding and fruit cocktail tasted great, but when chased with a mug of strong, black coffee and followed immediately by more hard riding—it seemed there was a hill out of every checkpoint—this food wouldn't digest, it would ferment. The result was 24 hours of heartburn, burps and sporadic hiccups. Luckily, this distress stayed above the waistband.

It also helped keep me awake through the long, chilly second night. Having napped for two hours in Brest that morning, my goal was to reach Paris before sleeping again. Thus far, I was way ahead of my most optimistic schedule, having reached the 380-mile halfway point in 23:15 (18.2 mph average riding speed) thanks to a tailwind, fresh legs and the motivation of having hundreds of 90-hour riders to pass. (They had started 7 hours ahead of my 84-hour group.) My goal of 65 hours seemed well within reach, even though the return trip would be tougher due to the sun, wind, elevation gain and increasing fatigue.

I rolled away from the Atlantic in the company of Paul Chandler, a strong rider from Baltimore. A member of an earlier group, he'd just had seven hours of sleep and was happy to set the pace. Streaming toward us were hundreds of riders enjoying the gale that was now in our face, holding us to less than 16 mph. And so it went for this long, sun-baked day. We even had to pedal on descents or lose speed.

Soon after leaving the Carhaix checkpoint, we caught North Carolina's John Lee Ellis, the Ultra-Marathon Cycling Association's perennial mileage champion (28,200 in 1990). A 90-hour starter, he was riding PBP not to compete but as part of two weeks of seeing France—which he did by being on the bike almost all of the 14 days. He made us a three-some, and I was glad. His conversation and strength were as good as Chandler's.

And much better than mine. Although I felt fine upon mounting up in Brest, my legs had no zip. I could hang in, but pulling was real work. Still, the three of us passed scores of riders. At 10:40 P.M. we arrived at the Fougeres checkpoint, having ridden 191 miles since Brest at an average of 15.2 mph. We ate together, then I thanked them for their help as they went to sleep and I went to ride. One hundred and eighty-nine miles remained.

A Hard Day's Night

Now I'm on my own. The hiccups return as I climb aboard, and a semisolid burp comes during the lengthy ascent from town. I'm cussing about it and feeling extra ornery as I overtake a French rider. I don't want company, but he sticks with me over the top, and we begin trading pulls. Suddenly, my legs feel better than they have all day. A burnt-orange moon has risen to silver, the terrain is relatively flat, and the headwind is but a breeze. Soon there are four of us, then six, flying through the night toward the Villaines checkpoint, some 45 miles away.

I'm not sure whether these guys know the road or are just nuts, but they begin blasting through blind, downhill curves that have no painted lines to mark the edge of the pavement. The coarse surface doesn't have potholes, though, and I haven't seen roadkill all day, so I fasten my seat belt and join in. In fact, I get so into it I drop them on a climb and solo for 30 minutes, enjoying a senseless euphoria that just can't last. My gut churns, and they catch me when I stop to get out the Gas-X.

Cruelly, the gale starts ripping again. God, it's 2:00 A.M.! What kind of place is this where wind pours all night from a star-filled sky? We begin riding raggedly, pounding hard and weaving dangerously, rear wheels flashing in and out of the beam behind. I move to the side, choosing to buck the air rather than risk a crash. A tall rider with sinewy legs is already there. I can't see his face, but based on his body and what looks like blond hair, I imagine he is a 25-year-old Swede.

For some reason he decides to pedal harder and I get on his wheel, followed by the four others. Accelerating smoothly, he shifts up once, twice, and when I glance back only one rider remains. Streetlights, and we're in Villaines, whaling through the narrow, curving streets between centuries-old stone buildings, rumbling across cobbled cross-walks, and paying no heed to stop signs. Now we are two. As we round a downhill corner at criterium speed, I'm think-ing this guy must know something I don't. Then I see the control banner stretched across the street and let up, al-lowing him the reward he is after: cheers from a dozen young boys and handshakes from men he obviously knows.

But wait, this is no young Swede. The blond hair is actually gray and worn by a Frenchman about my age, 45. He smiles at me as we park our bikes and walk unsteadily to a large room with a wooden floor ringed by sponsorship banners. In a scene that Fellini would admire, ten silent Frenchmen sit attentively at the long table. It's 3:18 A.M. We are the only riders here. They greet us pleasantly but with an air of decorum, which also describes the way the French run every aspect of PBP. It's professional, polite and above all, important. Things are done according to protocol. As I'm thinking about this, my new friend buys me a large cup of hot, black coffee. My gut will hate me for it, but what the hell.

With our former companions wrapped in blankets and reclining in lawn chairs beside their support van (this really is surreal), the two of us leave town. He's still dressed in shorts and a summer jersey, so he must be freezing—I know I am, and I'm wearing twice as much. That's probably why his headlight disappears behind me on the hill leaving town, even though I'm barely turning my 39 × 26T low gear. The hiccups start again.

For a while I'm alone in open, rolling farmland, no lights fore or aft. I try to remember coming through here in day-light but can't. Just when I begin to fear that I have missed one of the large red-on-yellow arrows marking a turn, I come upon a trike, of all things, being pumped along by a bloke from England. His accent makes me recall a comment from another Brit some 24 hours earlier as we scaled a hill together: "It's a bit more lumpy than I figgered." Lumpy. It was, and it is.

I feel I'm still making good time, even without the help of allies like Chandler, Ellis or glory-seeking Frenchmen. Dawn will break in two hours. It'll be interesting to see how much my average speed has increased overnight. . . .

Whoa! A headlight catches me so quickly I think it's a motorcycle. And in a sense it is—an 80-hour guy named James from New York who turns out to be cycling's answer to a Harley 883. I've ridden with some gear mashers in my day, but no one who could move a bike across flat ground or down a hill like Jimbo. And as he would settle onto his aero bar and try to break his crank, I swear I could hear him whistling.

We stay together almost to the Mortagne checkpoint, where he stops short at a support van for more of his liquid diet while I climb a hill I will never forget. In the cold, gray dawn, it was a killer curving upward with a particularly nasty pitch to the checkpoint's doorway. Give me a break! I scan my computer to see that my elapsed time is 50:38 and I've climbed 27,560 feet in 673 miles. But I'm dumbstruck to find that my average speed since Brest has dropped to 14.6 mph. What an illusion the night has been. All that speed with the Frenchman into Villaines, James's mighty pulls, my concerted solo efforts—just slow motion made fast by darkness, wind, fatigue and a hopeful imagination.

At least I can console myself with the fact that no one but James has caught me in the last 100 miles. And as I leave Mortagne ahead of him, I silently vow that he won't catch me again. With only 92 miles to go, it's time to use whatever is left.

And I do, passing about 20 more riders on the road to the finish, including half a dozen with frame numbers indicating they're in my 84-hour group. Neither James nor anyone else comes up from behind. As an old time trialist, this is important to me. There may be only one PBP in my life, and good memories depend on beating people and having a good time (clock) even more than a good time (experience). But I had both, arriving at 57:38 to finish seventh of the 600 or so cyclists in my group. Among all American single-bike riders, I trailed only Dickson and Hearst. This placed me 57th of 2,618 official finishers. It just shows what dedicated training and a stubborn attitude are worth.

But for many who would finish behind me and cry just as deeply, it was not a matter of how fast but the completion of the task. They—no we—are anciens, and for this we received a medal exactly like the one awarded to the winners. Fittingly, exact finishing times are engraved in small, inconspicuous type as if to acknowledge that everyone who beats the overall time limit, whether by a day or a minute, deserves equal acclaim.

Qualifications for PBP

It's not exactly racing, but it's a far cry from touring, It's randonnee cycling, from the French word *randonnee*, meaning "ramble," and nowhere is the concept better defined than by Paris-Brest-Paris.

Originated in 1891, the 1,200-kilometer event has endured to become cycling's oldest. Counting 1991's centennial edition there have been a dozen, though only since 1971 has PBP adhered to a consistent, quadrennial schedule.

The ride pits each participant, or randonneur, against a hilly, rural course that varies slightly each time, but the distance and time limits are always the same. Riders have a window within which to reach various checkpoints (also called controls). Some are unannounced to prevent shortcuts, and riders must complete the entire distance within a prescribed time. Randonneurs can choose to be in one of three groups, aiming to finish within 80, 84 or 90 hours. If a rider arrives at a control or the end even one minute late, he or she is disqualified.

PBP's centennial saw the largest field ever, with 3,281 randonneurs, from 24 countries, leaving Paris. Only 80 percent made it back. With 398 starters, the United States had the largest foreign contingent, as it did in 1987 (230) and 1983 (107). But compared with the last PBP when almost half quit, the Americans redeemed themselves with 340 official finishers. As always, obtaining a chance to participate entailed more than sending an entry fee. Much more.

To ride PBP you must qualify through a series of shorter events called brevets. Held in 24 regions throughout the United States and Canada, these include rides of 200, 300, 400 and 600 kilometers (124, 186, 248 and 372 miles), with controls and overall time limits of 14, 20, 27 and 40 hours, respectively. These events are designed to acquaint randonneurs with PBP protocol and introduce ever-longer distances, extremes in weather, nutritional challenges, night riding and sleep deprivation. As brevets lengthen, perseverance and self-sufficiency become as important to success as strength and conditioning.

All brevets are governed by rules of the International Randonneurs, the North American affiliate of the worldwide organization, Randonneurs Mondiaux. For newcomers, PBP qualification is based on completion of the brevet series during the year before and year of the event, or during the event year alone if an extra, 1,000-kilometer (620-mile) brevet is ridden within 75 hours. In addition, a North American cousin of PBP, the 750-mile Boston-Montreal-Boston (BMB), is held most years the French event is not and serves as an optional qualifier.

For more information on PBP and randonneuring, contact director James L. Konski, International Randonneurs, 727 N. Salina St., Syracuse, NY 13208; (315) 471-2101. For BMB, contact Charles Lamb, Box 721, Burlington, MA 01803; (617) 354-2887.

2 BECOME A PART OF CYCLING HISTORY

Fame may be fleeting, but it's not only for the fleet. You don't have to win the Tour de France six times or break the world hour record to become part of cycling's ledger of fame. With a little ingenuity in choosing a record attempt, nearly any fit cyclist can etch his or her name beside those of history's most revered riders . . . sort of.

Most of the official records of the U.S. Cycling Federation (USCF) and the worldwide Union Cycliste International (UCI) are reserved for elite riders using equally elite equipment. The inside track to immortality lies in serious but overlooked niches, many of them involving long distances. This book will show you how to extend your endurance; this chapter might give you some ideas for capitalizing on it.

Cincinnati cyclist Paul Liebenrood is one rider who did just that. "In 1984 the U.S. amateur hour record was one that didn't receive a lot of attention," he recalls. "I only thought about breaking it because a friend of mine held it." In September of that year at the Major Taylor Velodrome in Indianapolis, Liebenrood covered slightly more than 45 kilometers in an hour to become part of cycling history.

His record has long since been eclipsed—the current USCF hour mark is John Frey's 49.946 kilometers—but his record-setting experience can never be taken away.

John Marino, cofounder of the Ultra-Marathon Cycling Association (UMCA) and the former holder of several marks, explains the lure of record-chasing: "We all get old and will be forgotten. But you can leave a sort of legacy. Even if a record you set is broken, anyone who looks at history will know that at one time you were the best."

Where might your niche lie? First, forget about UCI fame unless your mother's maiden name is Merckx or LeMond. Instead, consider a USCF record. A one-wheel, juggling double century won't count, though. You must ride one of the standard events listed in the USCF rule book. But ignore high-profile ones such as the 40-kilometer time trial, because the speed is simply beyond the reach of most of us.

Amazingly, however, no attempts have been made on a number of USCF record categories, particularly border-to-border rides. Any of these might be to you what the amateur hour was to Liebenrood in 1984. (See the list of possibilities beginning on page 18.)

Another strategy would be to plan your attempt far in advance—say 40 years or so. USCF records are divided into age groups, and you're bound to face less competition at 70 than at 30.

But even if you have the right stuff to set a USCF record, you might not have the green stuff. USCF assistant executive director John Tarbert estimates that meeting the organization's requirements of membership, three official witnesses, electronic timing, drug testing and possibly velodrome rental can cost $1,000 to $4,000.

Smaller, specialty organizations such as the UMCA and the International Human-Powered Vehicle Association (IHPVA) offer less stringent record-setting alternatives, and the cost of making an attempt at this level is generally cheaper. But like the USCF, they accept challenges only in existing categories.

Cyclists are also recognized by the *Guinness Book of World Records*. But getting into *Guinness* can be tougher than cracking the USCF ranks. "We don't consider fad records," explains Mark Young, editor of the U.S. edition. "Nor do we consider specific activities where you're the only person who's ever performed that event, or dangerous stunts." (This may explain why the book years ago deleted the record for eating a bicycle.) "Practically the only way in," says Young, "is to beat an existing record."

He also says that activities without a governing body are rarely considered (one reason you won't see in-line skating records, for example). This can be bad news for some creative riders.

Consider the case of a couple of cycling friends, David Kerner and Scott Printz. After driving 900 miles in one day and passing through only two states, they decided to find a route that would let them cycle through as many states as possible in 24 hours. They now hold, as far as anyone can tell, the record for such a feat: six states in 16 hours, 40 minutes (200 miles through Maine, New Hampshire, Vermont, Massachusetts, Connecticut and Rhode Island).

So if your destiny is an unofficial cycling record, follow the lead of Kerner and Printz and choose an exploit that's barely beyond the average mortal's ability (and sense of decorum). Basing your record just past reality will make it seem extraordinary yet attainable, a combination that makes it memorable.

Most of these personal gauntlets are staged as charity benefits or publicity stunts. To gain media coverage, alert as many local newspapers and TV and radio stations as you can. Smaller stations might even provide live coverage, especially if you're cycling for charity. And, of course, hold your attempt in as public a place as possible. Start/finish lines in front of town hall or in public parks, festivals or shopping malls are ideal.

Finally, maybe the most important advice for turning your dreams of recognition into reality: "Never," advises Kerner, "do a record challenge that you accept on New Year's Eve."

Long-Distance Records You Can Set

Your ticket to glory might lie in any of the following goals that are ripe for the ambitions of the right cyclist.

- Individual men's transcontinental crossing (UMCA). The coast-to-coast mark of seven days, 23 hours, 16 minutes was set by Michael Secrest in 1990. Pete Penseyres covered 198.5 more miles with a time of eight days, 9 hours and 47 minutes in 1986.
- Two-man team transcontinental crossing (UMCA). Lon Haldeman and Pete Penseyres had a time of seven days, 14 hours, 55 minutes in 1987.
- Four-man team transcontinental crossing (UMCA). Team Manheim crossed in six days, 37 minutes in 1991.
- Individual women's transcontinental crossing (UMCA). Susan Notorangelo: nine days, 9 hours, 9 minutes in 1989.
- Two-woman team transcontinental crossing (UMCA). Estelle Grey and Cheryl Marek set a record of ten days, 22 hours, 48 minutes in 1984.
- Four-woman team transcontinental crossing (UMCA). Unestablished.
- Individual men's border-to-border crossing (USCF). Scott Hitchman's ride of five days, 20 hours, 27 minutes from Canada to Mexico has stood since 1983. (UMCA) Michael Shermer: three days, 23 hours, 49 minutes (West Coast), Victor Gallo: five days, 19 hours, 56 minutes (East Coast), 1989.

- Two-man team border-to-border crossing (USCF). Unestablished.
- Four-man team border-to-border crossing (USCF). Unestablished.
- Individual women's border-to-border crossing (USCF). Unestablished. (UMCA) Elaine Mariole: four days, 22 hours, 1 minute (West Coast), 1984.
- Two-woman team border-to-border crossing (USCF) (UMCA). Unestablished.
- Four-woman team border-to-border crossing (USCF) (UMCA). Unestablished.
- 24-hour men's roller ride (measured by "distance" according to roller revolutions) (UMCA). Richard Gunther travelled 853.46 miles with an average speed of 35.56 mph. 1990.
- 24-hour women's roller ride (UMCA). Cheryl Marek travelled 500.6 miles with an average speed of 20.86 mph. 1990.
- 24-hour unpaced time trial (IHPVA). Australian Gerry Tatrai rode 503.73 miles in 1991 just a week after finishing third in the Race Across America.
- State crossings (UMCA). Border-to-border records exist for 24 states (Alabama, Arizona, California, Colorado, Delaware, Florida, Kansas, Illinois, Indiana, Maryland, Massachusetts, Montana, New York, North Carolina, Ohio, Oklahoma, Oregon, South Carolina, Texas, Vermont, Virginia, Washington, Wisconsin and Wyoming). The remaining 26 states are records waiting to be established.
- Reno to Tucson (UMCA). Ed Levinson of Oakland rode the 849 miles from city hall to city hall in 72 hours, 20 minutes.
- Miami to Atlanta (UMCA). Victor Gallo of Miami rode 710 miles from city hall to city hall in 49 hours, 45 minutes.
- Austin-Houston-Austin (UMCA). Lynn Schmerhorn of Houston rode the 332 miles in 34 hours, 59 minutes in 1988.
- Portland to Salt Lake City (UMCA). Ray Youngberg of Salem, Oregon, was 52 in 1987 when he rode 785 miles from Oregon to Utah in 64 hours, 40 minutes.

(Note: The UMCA recognizes many other city-to-city and point-to-point records. New rides won't receive approval unless they involve significant start/end points.)

Finally, there's the unofficial record from the Capitol Building in Washington, D.C., to Baltimore city hall. In 1936, Ed Bieber rode the 37.5 miles in one hour, 34 minutes, 31 seconds. His average speed of about 24 mph seems beatable. But at least 30 cyclists, including a French pro, have challenged the record and failed, adding to its mystique. Increased traffic is blamed.

For more information on the record requirements of the organizations mentioned, contact:

Guinness Book of World Records, Facts on File, 460 Park Ave. South, New York, NY 10016.

International Human-Powered Vehicle Association, Box 51255, Indianapolis, IN 46251-0255; (317) 876-9478.

Ultra-Marathon Cycling Association, 2761 N. Marengo, Altadena, CA 91001; (818) 794-3119.

U.S. Cycling Federation, 1750 E. Boulder St., Colorado Springs, CO 80909; (719) 578-4581.

Part Two

POSITION AND TECHNIQUE

3 SOLUTIONS TO SADDLE SORES

It's the final week of long-distance training for your first double century. Everything has been going great. Your bike is in top shape, your confidence is high and the weather for the event is supposed to be perfect. But suddenly you're finding it hard to get comfortable on the saddle.

The problem began when you climbed on the bike this morning, and now it's all you can think about. Every bump in the road causes a stab of pain. Oh, no—all your preparation is being undermined by a saddle sore.

This term is loosely applied to any skin damage where you sit, but most often it is an infection that begins as a small, pimplelike bump on your crotch (the skin between your legs or on the lower portion of your rear end). In most cases, a saddle sore's life span is just a few days. But in this time, it may become hard, red, inflamed and quite painful. In some cases, the infection doesn't disappear. It spreads to adjacent tissue and creates larger sores, boils or cysts that affect more tissue and may even require surgery. To prevent this, proper treatment is required.

The crotch area is a perfect breeding ground for bacteria. It's warm and moist, and the glands in the skin secrete fluid that is rich in fat and other nutrients. Normally, several kinds of bacteria live harmlessly on the surface. But cycling changes all this. It causes pressure and irritation that can force the bacteria through the skin's protective outer layers into the sensitive inner ones where they flourish. After the bacteria penetrate the skin in this way, a saddle sore usually begins to form.

When that happens, your body builds an impermeable barrier around the site. Usually, that would seal it off from the rest of the body. Cycling, however, interferes with this. When you ride, you sit on the sore, putting pressure on the protective barrier and possibly causing it to rupture. When a saddle sore bursts, its contents are spilled into the surrounding tissue, and the infection spreads. If this recurs, the result can be a large boil or cyst.

As long as saddle sores are small they don't present any immediate hazard to your health. They are simply an uncomfortable inconvenience. But if they turn into larger sores or boils, they can cause scarring and permanent skin damage. Cysts are even worse. These hard lumps are easily reinfected and often must be removed surgically, as happened to Irish pro Sean Kelly in one Tour of Spain. Because of a cyst, Kelly, who was leading the race, was forced to quit.

To lessen the chance of getting saddle sores, follow these six tips.

1. Wear padded cycling shorts, but not underwear. The liner in the crotch helps reduce heat and friction, keeping bacterial growth to a minimum.
2. Wash your shorts after every use. You should have at least two pairs so you always have one clean for a ride.
3. If at all possible, dry the shorts inside-out in the sun. The benefit: Ultraviolet radiation kills bacteria.
4. Except when you're riding, wear loose-fitting pants. By increasing air circulation and keeping the crotch area dry between rides, loose-fitting clothes help reduce bacterial growth. Sleeping without underwear may also help.

5. Wash regularly with an antibacterial soap. Hibi-clens and Betadine Surgical Scrub are two non-prescription brands, available at drugstores. Using one of these products daily will reduce bacterial growth and your chances of developing saddle sores. (Regular soap doesn't help, because it has no antibacterial ingredients.)
6. Check your saddle height. An incorrectly posi-tioned saddle can cause chafing in the crotch area, which then becomes especially susceptible to in-fection. To minimize the risk, keep your saddle at the right height. Also, keep the saddle parallel to the top tube. If the nose is angled upward, it will put undue pressure on your crotch.

If despite these suggestions you do get a saddle sore, the best initial treatment is to wash the area a couple of times a day with antibacterial soap. Then keep it as dry as possible. Apply talcum or baby powder before riding to re-duce friction, which helps keep the sore from spreading.

Don't cover the sore with salves or ointments, because these may actually keep the bacteria alive. Also, don't apply alcohol. It can dry the skin and cause cracking and addi-tional irritation that may lead to even more sores.

Since saddle sores by definition are in hard-to-see ar-eas, use a mirror to monitor the sore. If it grows, hardens or persists for more than a few days, continue the washings and stay off your bike for a couple of days. If the sore is still there in a week, see a dermatologist.

An Emergency Fix for Saddle Sores

If an important ride like that double century is at hand, you certainly don't want a saddle sore to stop you. One way to significantly reduce the pressure and pain is to surround the sore with a donut cut from a section of Dr. Scholl's Molefoam, available in the foot-care section of drugstores. Make the center hole large enough to accommodate the sore. This trick is used by ultramarathon riders, who often fill the center with Boil Ease, a nonprescription ointment that has a topical painkiller and causes the sore to drain. The Molefoam's adhesive backing will keep it in place, even in moist conditions.

4 HAND POSITIONS

Perhaps no malady is more common among long-distance cyclists than numb or tingling fingers. A similar condition, known as carpal tunnel syndrome, has been making news in the workplace, afflicting employees who do repetitive tasks with their hands. In cycling, the problem is known as ulnar neuropathy or handlebar palsy. It occurs as pressure on the handlebar compresses the ulnar nerve, which passes from the forearm through the heel of the hand. The numbness is usually temporary, but in some cases it becomes chronic and surgery is required.

To reduce the pressure, you can wear padded or gel-filled gloves and/or use padded handlebar wrap. But there's an even better way, and that's to change your grip on the bar frequently by using the positions shown in the photos beginning on page 26. This is also helpful for general upper-body comfort, because each new grip changes the extension of your arms, unlocking your elbows and altering the angle of your neck and lower back to allay stiffness.

In addition, your hands are important for effective climbing, sprinting and flatland riding. Each situation requires a different grasp for efficiency and comfort. Fortunately, the common drop bar provides an elegant, simple solution, offering seven basic positions and infinite variations. No matter which you are using, always keep two fingers closed around the bar or brake hoods to prevent losing control on bumps.

(Note: Cycling gloves have been removed for these photos to make hand positions easier to see, but they are highly recommended. In addition to their protective padding, they absorb sweat to ensure a secure grip, eliminate raw spots and blisters and prevent abrasion in a fall.)

1. Both hands on the top. This position is best for sustained seated climbing or when pushing hard at less than 16 mph. In these instances the ability to leave the chest unconstricted and breathe freely is more important than aerodynamic efficiency. However, since braking is impossible, don't follow others too closely or use this grip in a pack.

Grasp the bar about two inches from either side of the stem. A narrower grip sacrifices leverage and control, while a wider one splays the elbows and creates drag. Keep your wrists and elbows slightly bent. Hold the bar lightly, but don't forget to keep at least two fingers closed around it. For added power, pull with one arm while pushing with the opposite leg, then relax that arm. Greg LeMond favors this technique on steep climbs, rocking powerfully from side to side.

2. One hand on top. When removing one hand from the handlebar to eat, drink or stretch, place the other an

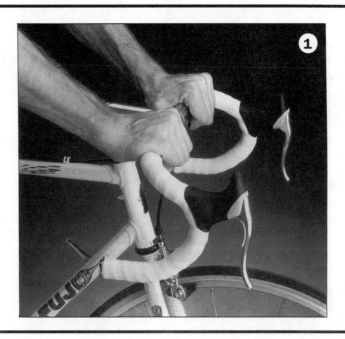

inch from the stem. This is the safest position because oversteering is less likely when the hand is close to the turning axis. Look at the road ahead first to ensure that the pavement is smooth and your hand won't be jarred loose. Don't use this position when riding in a pack.

   3.   On the hoods. (See page 28.) Like your favorite sofa, this is where you go to relax. It's more aerodynamic than riding on the tops, but still offers easy breathing. Use it for flatland cruising or when riding in a pack. It's also the best position for out-of-saddle climbing.

   Place your thumbs to the inside of the hoods and rest one or two fingers on the levers for quick braking. Rest the center of your palms on the bar's upper curves. Keep your elbows bent but not flared to the outside. When standing, close two fingers around the hoods for a firmer grip.

   To prevent cocking the wrists excessively, make sure the levers are correctly positioned. Here's the rule: A straightedge extended from beneath the bar should touch

the tip of the lever. The bottom of the bar should be level or pointed a few degrees down toward the rear hub.

4.   On the hoods with fingers split. (See opposite page.) This variation of grip number 3 is an excellent way to relieve pressure on the normal weight-bearing parts of the palms. It also facilitates bending the elbows to achieve a low, aero position. However, it makes braking impossible, so don't use it in a pack.

Place your index fingers to the inside of the hoods and rest the center of your palms on the bar's upper curves. Lightly close each thumb and one other finger around the bar.

5.   Palms on the hoods. (See page 30.) This position is another way to relieve pressure on the normal weight-bearing parts of the palms while allowing a low, aero posi-

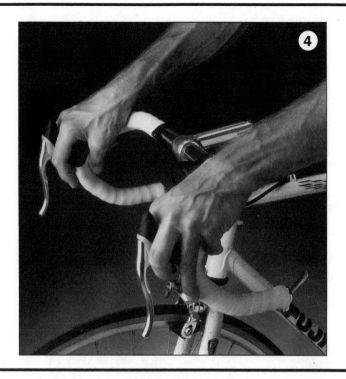

tion. But like grip number 1, it doesn't allow braking and shouldn't be used in a pack. It's also not comfortable for long periods because the hood peaks tend to press in.

Position the peaks roughly in the center of your palms. Bend your arms sharply to get low.

6.   On the drops. (See page 30.) This is what drop bars were made for, and it's the most aerodynamic position for fast flatland riding and descending. It's also good for short, powerful, out-of-saddle efforts such as sprinting or surmounting small hills. However, most riders find it's not comfortable for long and doesn't provide much climbing leverage. Use it at least a few times on every ride to develop the necessary flexibility and arm strength.

Rest the edge of your hands (below the pinkie) on the flat portion of the bar with the wrists straight. Keep your

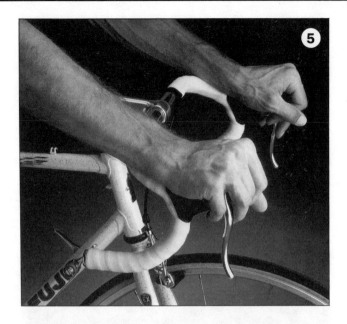

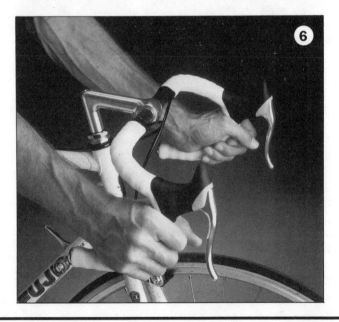

elbows bent and in line with your body. When riding in a pack, descending or cornering, keep one or two fingers on the levers for quick braking. During hard solo efforts, bend your arms more to get lower, but keep your head up.

Hand size can be accommodated by bars with different drops (the distance from the center of the bar top to the center of the flat bottom portion). Large drop is 16 centimeters; normal, 15 centimeters; shallow, 14 centimeters.

7. On the bottom of the hooks. This provides the same aero advantage as grip number 6 but offers a different grasp to alleviate hand numbness. It also allows you to use bar-end shifters with minimal movement. Disadvantages are that you lose access to the brakes, and your wrists can fatigue because they are more cocked. Keep your elbows in. To become more aero, bend the arms 90 degrees.

This position has one other use: time trial starts. Grasp the bottoms firmly, lock your arms, and push and pull with a rigid upper body to get maximum acceleration off the line.

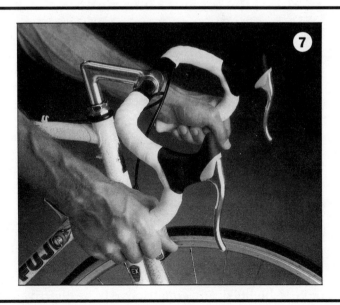

■5■ LONG-DISTANCE COMFORT

Have you tried long-distance events, only to find that they leave you uncomfortably stiff? Do your legs go weak? Is it your bike—or your riding position?

Try this experiment. Sit with your hands on your knees and tense your shoulders so they're up near your ears. Then extend your arms in front of you and lock your elbows. Now clench your fists. Hold this position.

Uncomfortable, right? Believe it or not, though, that's how most people ride. No wonder completing 75 or 100 miles is rough. Of course, the key to comfortable riding is a properly fitted bike. For pointers, visit a bike shop that's equipped with a professional sizing system such as the Fit Kit. Once you're set up correctly, here are some subtle (and some not-so-subtle) things you can do to make your long rides more comfortable.

Tips for the Long Haul

Although your bike will never be an armchair, a high degree of comfort is attainable. If not, it wouldn't be possible for professional cyclists to race six to eight hours a day for weeks at a time, and events such as Race Across America would be inconceivable.

Pro cyclists prefer a long reach (that is, a longer handlebar stem) and a relaxed frame geometry. The long stem helps keep their shoulders and back relaxed, while the shallower frame angles make for a smoother ride. Although such adaptations compromise responsiveness, they're crucial to riders who earn their living in the saddle.

For long-distance comfort it's also essential to minimize the friction between you and the bike. It's the contact points of the hands, feet and seat that need the most attention. The first step is wearing the proper clothing:

Padded cycling gloves absorb road shock. But they don't have to be bulky and constrictive to be effective. New gel materials and other substitutes for old-fashioned foam can be quite thin and still provide plenty of protection. Gloves should fit snugly, but not so tight that circulation is reduced.

Stiff-soled cycling shoes enhance pedaling efficiency and minimize foot fatigue. Fit is crucial, though. Unlike running shoes, there's no need for extra room in the toe box, but also the shoes shouldn't be too snug unless they're made of leather, which will stretch. (Synthetic materials don't.)

Cycling shorts with a padded liner reduce friction and add softness. Choose a synthetic liner rather than a natural chamois, which takes much longer to dry and quickly loses its suppleness. In general, it's better to pay more to get higher-quality shorts. Your comfort is worth it, and there will be less chance of a poor fit that leads to abrasion and saddle sores.

After your body is properly outfitted, check your bike. Even if you have a good overall fit, a few slight alterations can greatly enhance comfort.

First, your saddle must be adequate. If you're having trouble with it, make sure it's level and not excessively worn. Since there are subtle differences among saddles, experiment with various shapes until you find one that's right for you. Remember, though, that the saddle that's comfortable 100 percent of the time hasn't been invented yet.

Next, turn your attention to the handlebar. Many bikes come with bars that are 38-centimeters wide. But most average-size riders should have one that's 40 centimeters, and if you're big and broad shouldered, a 42-centimeter model will be even more comfortable.

Check the brake levers. The bottom tip of each brake lever should be aligned with the flat part of the handlebar drops (which, in turn, should be almost parallel to the ground). Hold a straightedge to the bottom of the drops to check this. Such a position ensures optimum accessibility and comfort. Then make sure to use the whole bar by changing your grip frequently, as discussed in chapter 4.

Relax those hands. While riding, keep in mind our stiff-shoulder experiment and how tiring it was to hold that position. Avoid grasping the handlebar in a death grip. With your palms on the bar, occasionally flutter your fingers. This will keep them light and relaxed, but ready to steer and brake.

Keep your elbows unlocked. Riding with stiff arms is not only fatiguing but also dangerous because it severely limits your ability to make subtle changes in direction. Crashes often occur in races when people tense up and lock their arms. Try steering with your elbows locked, then relax them and feel the difference for yourself.

Last, get those shoulders out of your ears! Most cyclists ride this way simply because they don't realize they're doing it. Videotaping is an inexpensive and graphic way to notice such things. All riders benefit from seeing themselves. Often it's the subtlest change in body position that yields the greatest results. But in order to make that all-important correction, you have to realize what you're doing wrong. The camera doesn't lie.

Change your position and/or riding style gradually, because sudden adjustments can strain muscles or joints. Reassess your progress periodically by videotaping or asking a training partner for his or her evaluation.

When you're on a long ride, think about your upper body as well as those strong, hard-working legs. Think of all the energy that a tense upper body wastes. Try to keep your back flat, and at least once every 30 minutes get out of the saddle and stretch your lower back. Relax by taking a deep breath and exhaling all the tension. As you do this, drop your shoulders, unlock your elbows and flutter your fingers. For the long haul, you'll be happy you did.

6 22 TIPS FOR STRONGER CLIMBING

The longer the ride, the more you benefit by being a stronger, more efficient cyclist. And nowhere is the payoff greater than in the hills. In many parts of the country, a century ride may include a mile or more of vertical gain, putting a premium not only on strength but also on technique and equipment.

Like getting rich and losing weight, climbing better is something we'd all like to do. And come to think of it, having a few extra dollars and shucking several pounds can help you get uphill faster, too. Here's how, along with 20 other proven tips from *Bicycling* editors who ride in the abrupt terrains of eastern Pennsylvania and northern California. Apply them to your own climbing and watch your speed and endurance increase.

1. Lighten your bike. Climbing is mainly a fight with gravity, so anything you do to reduce the weight of your equipment will make hills easier. Lightness should be a priority when you shop for replacement parts, accessories or new components. For example, compared to a gel-padded saddle, the titanium-rail Selle Italia Flite model saves about half a pound. Replacing both hubs' steel quick-release skewers with an alloy version spares some three ounces. Having your next pair of wheels built with alloy spoke nipples rather than brass will save almost four ounces, and you can also choose lighter rims, spokes and tires if your weight, road conditions and wallet allow. And, of course, remove any unnecessary equipment and cargo before a hilly ride.

2. Lighten up your body. If you're overweight, you're reducing your climbing potential. The easiest way to increase VO_2 max, the key measurement of aerobic strength, is to decrease body weight. To illustrate how lightness can improve climbing speed, cycling expert Chester Kyle, Ph.D., created a computer model. It consisted of a course with a steep one-mile climb (10 percent slope) followed by a mile-long descent. A rider/bike weighing 180 pounds finished 22 seconds ahead of one 6 pounds heavier, which equates to a distance of 289 feet. Even on a milder 4 percent slope, the advantage was 166 feet. In reality, the distances gained might be greater because this model was based only on weight. Amplifying the benefit would be a rider's improved efficiency, as the pounds come off the person rather than the bike.

3.   Inflate tires to maximum pressure. You'll ascend quicker on narrow, high-pressure tires, but only if they're fully inflated. Check the sidewalls for maximum recommended pressure, then pump up before each hilly ride. This will minimize the size of your tires' contact patch with the road and significantly reduce rolling resistance. For example, a 175-pound rider on a 25-pound bike will roll almost 5 percent easier after increasing tire pressure from 75 to 110 psi.

4.   Reduce wind resistance. The slower you go, the less important an aerodynamic riding position becomes, but it's still worth something. You always create more frontal area when you're standing compared to sitting, and sitting upright compared to leaning forward. We know that about 70 percent of the drag in cycling is caused by the body's resistance to air, so compact riders expend less energy. Sit and use the lowest upper-body position that doesn't compromise breathing and comfort.

5.   Begin the climb in a lower gear than you need. This is especially important on long hills. By starting the ascent in a gear that lets you spin lightly, your muscles will be spared for the harder work ahead. You'll either be able to maintain a good cadence in the same gear, or shift to the next higher one and really make time. Meanwhile, those who began in a relatively high gear will fatigue, grope for an easier cog, and seem to be going backward as you spin by. What coaches tell racers is good advice for everyone: Climbing is a matter of shifting to higher gears, not lower ones.

6.   Shift up when you stand, down when you sit. Because you can't pedal as fast when standing, shift to the next higher gear (smaller rear cog) on the stroke before you rise from the saddle. Then your speed won't decrease much as your cadence slows. Conversely, shift to the next lower gear (larger cog) on the first stroke after sitting. Your faster cadence in the easier gear will maintain your speed.

7.   Sit rather than stand. On all but short "sprinter's hills," you will climb faster and more efficiently if you stay in the saddle. Standing makes your legs, arms and back work extra to support your body, and this increases use of oxygen and energy. A few strokes out of the saddle, however, can help relieve muscle fatigue in the midst of a long hill, and on steep pitches you may need to stand to keep the crank turning. But when given the choice, stay seated.

8.   Avoid macho gears. Senior *Bicycling* editor Don Cuerdon offers this advice: "Everyone who rides long distances in hill country should consider triple chainrings. It's impossible to learn good climbing technique when every hill is tantamount to a weight workout and you're above your anaerobic threshold. Since changing my 42 × 21T low to 39 × 23T or even 26T, I'm climbing faster."

9.   Grip the hoods, not the hooks. You're almost always a better climber with your hands atop the handlebar than on the lower portion. When standing, place your hands on the brake lever hoods (exception: sprinter's hills that can be charged over in the drops). Otherwise, bending into the drops may compress your diaphragm to the point where deep breathing is difficult. This position also makes it tough to look up the hill. When sitting, grip the hoods or bar top before it curves forward. Keeping your hands farther apart will aid steering and help open your chest for freer breathing. Bend your elbows to stay reasonably low.

10.   Don't strangle the bar. A firm grip is unnecessary at climbing's slow speed and only tenses your arm muscles. When standing, rest the crotch of your hands on the hoods and drape your fingers. When sitting and gripping the bar top, place your thumbs above so it's harder to forget and begin squeezing. Use a more secure grip, however, if the road is bumpy.

11.   Sway the bike when standing. While making sure not to veer, let the bike move side to side beneath you to receive a direct thrust from each leg. Like a metronome, this helps establish a rhythm that makes the climbing effort feel natural and easier. When your gear is right you'll know why this technique is described as "running on the pedals."

12.   Shift before the hill. During a long, rolling ride, considerable energy can be spared with timely shifts to maintain a consistent cadence. When you slow even slightly before shifting, it disrupts your rhythm, causing you to pedal harder briefly before clicking into a lower gear and spinning back up to speed. No cyclist can do it perfectly every time (that's why they invented motorcycles), but by anticipating shifts you'll be stronger in undulating terrain.

13.   Don't bounce your body (much). Some riders will tell you to climb with a quiet upper body—no rocking, bobbing or bouncing. It's true that excessive movement wastes energy, but so does trying to resist all motion. And it makes you slower. Instead, be natural. If you're active on the bike (like former Olympic champion Alexi Grewal), fine. If you're as still as Motorola pro Andy Hampsten, great. Let your body find its natural rhythm as you pull lightly on the bar to oppose leg thrusts.

14.   Synchronize your breathing. Just when you need air most, the exertion of climbing may cause you to pant or hold your breath. To remedy this, blend breathing with the rhythm of climbing by inhaling through your nose and/or mouth and exhaling forcefully through your mouth. This method provides ample oxygen and soon becomes ingrained. It also helps prevent tense jaw and neck muscles.

15.   Fasten your feet. When a big climb looms, tighten your shoe or toe straps. The firmness will make you feel powerful and, in fact, you will be able to push and pull more forcefully without fear of feet yanking free from pedals or sliding inside shoes. Later, slightly loosen the straps for greater cruising comfort.

16.   Reposition your seat. Determine your proper saddle height to make sure your position is correct. A study performed for the U.S. Cycling Federation found that an improperly set saddle increases oxygen consumption, with a slightly higher saddle being worse than a slightly lower one. If your height is off much, correct it by only a few millimeters per week to give your body time to adapt.

17.   Scoot your butt. By sliding to the rear of the saddle for harder sections of climbs, you effectively increase its height. This produces greater pedaling power at the expense of efficiency, but the trade-off is usually worth it for a few moments. Facilitate this position by gripping the bar top. At other times, particularly on short rises that you press over in the saddle, sliding forward can help you maintain your spin.

18.   Ride the shallow line. A sharp uphill curve can be ridden two ways (traffic permitting). A rider who uses the center of the road must cover a greater distance, but the pitch is noticeably shallower. Meanwhile, the few feet saved by a rider who hugs the inside of the curve doesn't offset the extra strain and loss of speed.

19.   Ride a straight line. The quickest path up any hill is one that avoids wiggles and wobbles. Weaving saps energy and scrubs speed. In fact, Kyle has found that even a one-degree steering angle increases rolling resistance about 6 percent. A three-degree variation from dead center raises it a whopping 30 percent. The reasons a rider has trouble maintaining a straight line include using too big a gear, gripping the bar too tightly, locking elbows and shoulders, and excessive upper-body movement. Relax and spin a low gear smoothly to keep your bike on track.

20.   When climbing with a group, ride at the front. This is key if you're not the strongest rider, and it's what road racers are taught. Sometimes, everyone will be content to ascend at your pace. But if they begin passing, maintain your comfortable speed and slowly drift back, hoping to remain with them over the top. If a gap opens, don't worry—you'll catch them on the descent if you haven't blown up in an anaerobic effort.

21.   Study good climbers. Talented ascenders will make all of these tips come to life. Watch them on club rides and try to duplicate their moves. Even better, offer to buy one lunch if he or she will spend an hour with you on the road, critiquing your style. If you can work with a coach in your area or attend a cycling camp, do it.

22.   Smile. Although a tough hill is rarely something to be happy about, grinning when you'd normally be grimacing can make you feel relaxed and confident. It's a simple trick, but it works.

Part Three
TRAINING

7 A TRAINING GUIDE FOR CENTURY RIDES

Linda Apriletti of Coral Gables, Florida, would like to forget her first century. Her bike weighed almost 30 pounds. She got lost. She ran out of food. "I just felt miserable," she recalls.

A few months later, she completed her second 100-miler. Her new 21-pound bike worked well. She paced herself. She had plenty to eat and drink. "It was a completely different experience," she says.

Like many other novice century riders, Apriletti learned the hard way how to prepare for a 100-mile event. But your first century needn't be a lesson in pain and frustration. By following a few simple guidelines, you can avoid common mistakes and have an enjoyable experience. If you're a veteran century rider, the following tips can help you achieve a personal best time.

The basis of successful century riding is training. With this in mind, we present *Bicycling*'s ten-week training schedules, which have been proven effective by thousands of riders since they were introduced in 1986. Schedule 1, designed for cyclists attempting their first century, is geared for those who've been riding an average of 45 to 50 miles a week. If you've been riding a bit more, increase the distances slightly. Use schedule 2 if you've been cycling more than 75 miles a week. It will help you finish your first century comfortably, or set a new personal best.

In both charts, "easy" means taking a leisurely ride, "pace" means matching the speed you plan to maintain for the century and "brisk" means cycling faster than your century pace. If your century ride is on Saturday, move back the final week's training one day (that is, take Wednesday off and ride ten miles on Thursday and five on Friday).

No matter which schedule you follow, you'll need to find time to train during the week. Try commuting to work, riding at lunch, using an indoor resistance trainer and so forth. Though it's possible to prepare for a century by riding just four days a week, a six-day schedule works best. Remember that easy riding facilitates recovery better than does inactivity.

With both schedules, Saturday is crucial. Doing progressively longer distances each weekend is the key to a successful century. It's wise to schedule your long ride for

Ten-Week Century Training Schedule #1

Week	Mon. Easy	Tues. Pace	Wed. Brisk	Thurs.	Fri. Pace	Sat. Pace	Sun. Pace	Total Weekly Mileage
1	6	10	12	Off	10	30	9	77
2	7	11	13	Off	11	34	10	86
3	8	13	15	Off	13	38	11	98
4	8	14	17	Off	14	42	13	108
5	9	15	19	Off	15	47	14	119
6	11	15	21	Off	15	53	16	131
7	12	15	24	Off	15	59	18	143
8	13	15	25	Off	15	65	20	153
9	15	15	25	Off	15	65	20	155
10	15	15	25	Off	10	5 Easy	Century	170

Ten-Week Century Training Schedule #2

Week	Mon. Easy	Tues. Pace	Wed. Brisk	Thurs.	Fri. Pace	Sat. Pace	Sun. Pace	Total Weekly Mileage
1	10	12	14	Off	12	40	15	103
2	10	13	15	Off	13	44	17	112
3	10	15	17	Off	15	48	18	123
4	11	16	19	Off	16	53	20	135
5	12	18	20	Off	18	59	22	149
6	13	19	23	Off	19	64	24	162
7	14	20	25	Off	20	71	27	177
8	16	20	27	Off	20	75	29	187
9	17	20	30	Off	20	75	32	194
10	19	20	30	Off	10	5 Easy	Century	184

this day so Sunday will be available in case of bad weather or other interruptions.

The goal is to increase mileage by 10 to 12 percent each week. If you simply want to complete the 100 miles, your longest training ride needn't exceed 65 miles. Even if your objective is to ride a fast-paced century, your longest ride won't have to be more than 75 miles.

Resist the temptation to boost your weekly mileage drastically, especially as the ride approaches. Overdoing it can lead to staleness, fatigue and injury. Watch for such overtraining warning signs as restless sleep, fluctuations in morning pulse rate, a sudden drop in weight, and fatigue or listlessness during workouts.

Do's and Don'ts for 100-Mile Efforts

There's more to successful century riding than adhering to training schedules. Here are 15 quick tips, with comments from several experienced long-distance riders. Use this advice to help make your century a fun and rewarding experience.

1.   Don't wait until you're thirsty to drink. On a warm day, drink as much as two bottles of liquid per hour. John D. Cook of Roseburg, Oregon, says he drinks half a bottle every ten miles. "I think water is the key to it," he says.

2.   Do drink before, during and after rides. This will avoid dehydration-induced fatigue. Harry Meyers of Diamond Springs, California, drank more than three gallons of liquid when he rode the Davis Double Century, but still got dehydrated. He says chicken soup helped him finish the 200 miles in about 17 hours.

3.   Do consider a carbohydrate-replacement energy drink. These specially designed mixtures will quench your thirst and supply vital glucose. In riding her second century, Apriletti used one and says, "It kept me from bonking."

4.   Do eat lots of carbohydrates. Eating pasta, rice or other high-carbohydrate dishes during the three days prior to the century boosts your reserves of glycogen, the primary muscle fuel. Try fruit, oatmeal, whole-grain cereal and bread for breakfast.

5.   Don't wait until you're hungry to eat during a long ride. Recommended snacks include bananas, cookies and dried fruit. Nibble something every ten minutes from the start, and your energy level will remain high.

6.   Don't stuff yourself. Eat lightly and steadily. Fill your pockets with food at rest stops, then eat while riding, rather than pig out on the spot.

7.   Do vary your riding position. Frequently move your hands from the top of the handlebar to the brake lever hoods to the drops. It'll prevent muscle fatigue.

8.   Do stretch while you ride. Every 30 minutes, stand on the pedals, arch your back and stretch your legs. To prevent upper body stiffness, do slow neck rolls and shoulder shrugs.

9.   Do divide the ride into segments and prepare a strategy for each. Don't get sucked into going at someone's faster pace. "Try to stay away from people who are trying to 'win' the century ride," says Apriletti.

   10.   Don't dwell on the miles remaining if you're getting tired. Instead, concentrate on form, efficiency, and drinking and eating adequately. "Give yourself plenty of time and try not to hurry," says Cook. "Just plan on finishing and enjoying it."

   11.   Don't stop for more than ten minutes. Longer rest breaks can make you stiff and sap your motivation.

   12.   Do make sure your bike is properly geared for the course. Ask the ride organizer or someone who's ridden the route previously for recommendations on the low gear you should have.

   13.   Do dress for comfort. Wear cycling shoes that fit comfortably, cycling shorts with a padded liner, and padded cycling gloves. Also, sunglasses protect your eyes and reduce fatigue from glare.

   14.   Do cycle with someone who has similar goals. "Ride with other people so you get support and encouragement," says Apriletti.

   15.   Do believe in yourself. Completing your first century or finishing one in personal record time is within your grasp. Think positive.

8 NINE DAYS TO GLORY

   A century ride is a test—of will, of fitness, of everything that goes into being a cyclist. This chapter presumes that you're now nine days from that test and ready to begin the final countdown. But first, let's look back at the weeks and months that have brought you to this point and quickly review how you've prepared (or should have) in three vital areas.

   Training. You put in the miles. Many riders follow a set program, such as the training schedules in chapter 7. These give daily instruction for ten weeks, beginning with weeks totaling 77 to 103 miles (depending on your goal) and building to 155 to 194 miles. Whether you followed our program or your own, it's crucial that as you near the big day, you have at least 1,000 miles and a trio of 50-mile rides in your legs.

Equipment. You got your bike into condition. Maybe you even bought an aero handlebar. That's good. An aero bar is the easiest way to lower your time. In fact, using one almost guarantees that you'll beat your best performance. The aerodynamic position lets you slice through the air with minimal frontal area. In addition, it's more comfortable for the long haul, easing the strain on your hands, arms, and back. It's best to install one as early in your training as possible, though, to give you time to master the tricky handling and accustom your body to the new position.

Nutrition. You focused on your diet. To fuel your training, you limited fat intake (nuts, sauces, dressings, ice cream, etc.) while increasing carbohydrate intake (fruit, bread, potatoes, pasta, etc.). You tried to keep your diet at 60 to 65 percent carbohydrate, 20 to 25 percent fat and 15 percent protein—the best mix for performance and health.

Now, with a mere nine days to go, don't think your preparation is over. Sure, it might seem too late to make any notable difference. But even if you've been to every class and read every chapter, you still have to study for the final exam. In fact, what you do in the next few days is crucial.

To ensure that your preparation is complete in each of the three key areas, adhere to the following schedule. Then you and your bike will be truly prepared for that singular moment when the preparation ends and the test begins.

Nine Days to Go

Training. Having completed the bulk of your conditioning, this is the time to set goals for the ride. By now you should have an idea of what kind of performance you can realistically expect. If it's your first century, just finishing should be your aim. If you're a veteran, set a specific time goal. For instance, for a five-hour century you must average 20 mph, so this is your target speed. For a six-hour century, it's 16.7 mph; for seven hours, 14.3 mph; for eight hours, 12.5 mph; for nine hours, 11.2 mph.

Pick your target and do a 15- to 20-mile ride at this speed. Afterward, take care of another key detail: If your century is out of town, make your hotel reservations. If it's a popular ride, do this even earlier. (For the sake of a good night's sleep, you're usually better off not staying with friends the night before.)

Equipment. While riding, listen to your bike. If you hear anything unusual, check it afterward. For instance, if you hear creaking when you climb, it may mean that your handlebar stem needs tightening, or it could signify a frame crack. In fact, even if there are no strange noises, it's a good idea to closely inspect your frame. Look at joints for hairline cracks. Such an imperfection could be disastrous.

Nutrition. Start paying attention to how your preride meals affect your performance. Some cyclists don't eat anything before a century. That's okay, as long as you eat well during the ride, the night before, and the few days prior. Others like to load up with a high-carbohydrate breakfast. This can work, too, as long as you allow enough time for digestion and don't eat too much. This is a good time to start deciding what your approach will be.

Eight Days to Go

Training. Today's ride is your dress rehearsal. Get into it—even wear your century clothes. While there's no need to ride a full 100, you should go 65 to 75 miles. Try for a negative split—riding the second half faster than the first—while averaging your target speed overall. If you can do this and still feel strong at the end, you're on track for a great century.

Equipment. Install a second water bottle cage. If your bike has seat tube braze-ons, put it there. If not, check local shops for a cage that piggybacks onto your existing one or attaches to the back of your saddle. If all this fails, at least use the largest water bottle you can find and plan to carry another in your jersey pocket.

Nutrition. Don't just carry the extra liquid, drink it liberally. During a multihour ride, you must replace the fluids used by your muscles and lost through sweating. To do this, drink at least one standard water bottle per hour—more if it's hot. Use this day's ride to get in the habit of sipping at regular intervals.

Seven Days to Go

Training. Recruit some friends for a 20- to 30-mile ride. Much of your century will likely be spent riding in a pack or paceline, so it's important to practice group riding skills—especially if you've been training alone. Stay within a wheel of the person in front of you, ride a straight line and avoid sudden movements. While group riding takes more concentration, it's worth it. Drafting saves about 1 percent of energy for each mile per hour you're traveling. So when you're drafting at 20 mph, you're expending 20 percent less energy than the rider leading the pack.

Equipment. Check the bearings in your hubs, bottom bracket and headset. (See chapter 19.) To test hub bearings, spin the wheels. They should move freely and slow gradually. To check the crank, take the chain off and spin the crankarms. They should turn without hesitation, odd clicks or bumps. To double-check, put one hand on each crankarm and push and pull them simultaneously. There shouldn't be any play. To check headset bearings, lift the front of the bike about six inches and drop it. If the handlebar area rattles, the bearings are loose. Another way is to stand beside the bike, squeeze the front brake and rock the bike to and fro, feeling for play between the fork and frame.

Nutrition. Decide on what kind of drink you'll use during the century. Energy drinks are almost essential for a 100-mile ride. During the mid portion, your glycogen (carbohydrate stores) will run out. Energy drinks are designed to quickly deliver fuel to the working muscles, allowing you to maintain the effort. You can buy these drinks at most bike shops and health food stores. If you've been experimenting with different brands, decide which one you'll use.

Six Days to Go

Training. Tailor this 15- to 20-mile ride to one thing: the century course. If it's flat, spend the ride on long straightaways. If it's rolling or hilly, train in a similar environment. The ideal situation is to drive the course, identify the toughest stretches, then ride them. Having already conquered a difficult climb or windy plain gives you a psychological edge when you encounter it on century day.

Equipment. Check your tires. Remove any stones, slivers of glass or other embedded items that could cause a flat. At the same time, check for wear. If you find any serious cuts or can't see the tread pattern, replace your tires. Also, check for loose spokes and spin the wheels to make sure they're true. If you plan to install a new set of tires or wheels for the century, don't wait any longer. You should ride with them at least once before the event.

Nutrition. Enter the carbo-load mode. To ensure that your glycogen stores are brimming for the century, begin increasing your carbohydrate intake. No matter how you've eaten to this point, it's crucial that your diet be 75 percent carbohydrate during the last week. Go for pasta, potatoes, fruit, Chinese food, bread. But hold the mayo—as well as other fatty foods.

Five Days to Go

Training. Think of this as weakness day. It's one of your last rides before the century, and you should spend it concentrating on your biggest flaw (climbing, cornering—whatever). This will help ease last-minute doubts. Ride 15 to 20 miles.

Equipment. Check that all your bike's bolts are tight. Also, inspect the cables for fraying, especially at the brake and shift levers. To test the brakes, squeeze the levers and see how quickly they snap back into position. If they stick or move slowly, your cables need to be lubricated or replaced. Inspect the brake pads for wear. The entire surface of the pad should touch the rim when the brakes are applied hard. If it doesn't, readjust.

Nutrition. To help load your muscles with glycogen, you may want to supplement your meals with a concentrated carbohydrate drink. Such products as Ultra Fuel, Exceed High Carbohydrate Source, and Gatorlode offer more than twice the percentage of carbohydrate as regular energy drinks. This heavy dose can hamper digestion during exercise, but they're ideal for building glycogen stores beforehand.

Four Days to Go

Training. This day marks a turning point in your training. Your chance to build fitness is behind you. Now it's time to taper, to gradually begin resting your body for the major effort that's only four days away. Before you slow down, however, give yourself one last good workout, riding 25 to 30 miles at a fast pace.

Equipment. Make sure shifting is responsive and positive. If you have an indexed "click shift" system and you've notice that shifts to larger cogs aren't as quick as they once were, turn the adjuster barrel (located where the cable/housing enters the derailleur) counterclockwise one-half turn. Conversely, if shifts to smaller cogs are slow, turn the barrel one-half turn clockwise. Turn and check performance until shifting is crisp in both directions.

Nutrition. Once you're within 100 hours of the century, increase your fluid intake. Make a point of consuming at least eight glasses of water a day. Your quadriceps and other leg muscles will need all that fluid to work efficiently for 100 miles.

Three Days to Go

Training. Take the day off. Any exercise you do will only lower your glycogen stores. If you still need training at this point, you're doomed.

Equipment. Clean the bike with a damp sponge and soft rag, even wax it—it'll make you feel fast. Lube the chain, derailleur and brake pivot points, and wipe off the excess. For a psychological lift, you may want to install new handlebar tape. It can serve as a constant reminder during the century that rehearsals are over, and this is the real thing.

Nutrition. As you carbo-load, don't make the mistake of eating too much. You don't want to acquire five extra pounds that'll slow you on the hills. Ingest your normal amount of calories, keeping the fat level low and the carbohydrate high. And keep drinking at least eight glasses of water a day.

Two Days to Go

Training. With the long-awaited weekend looming, take an easy ten-mile ride. Afterward, forget about the sport. Catch a movie, play with the kids, reintroduce yourself to your spouse. Researchers say such rest gives your muscles a needed opportunity to recover. Longtime cyclists claim the main advantage is mental— that after a day off, you come back sharper and more focused than before.

Equipment. Check your seat bag to make sure your tire repair kit is intact. You should carry a spare tube, three tire levers and a patch kit. Make sure the glue in the patch kit hasn't dried. And for emergencies, throw in some change and an ID card.

Nutrition. Because a century can last half the day, you'll probably crave solid food to go with your energy drink. Consider what you'll take to eat. The best are high-carbohydrate treats that fit in your jersey pocket and are easy to eat in the saddle. Some possibilities that you should have been experimenting with: energy bars, cookies (fig bars, oatmeal/raisin), bagels, muffins, bananas, dried fruit (raisins, figs, dates), pretzels, graham crackers and breadsticks. Deciding on these details in advance will minimize last-minute stress later.

One Day to Go

Training. Take an easy five-mile spin to relax and burn off nervous energy. On the eve of the ride, go to sleep early—but not too early. You'll perform more alertly if you stick with your normal resting pattern. If it's an out-of-town ride, make sure you arrive the day before the race. Having a long drive on the morning of the event will leave you tired and stiff in the second half of the century.

Equipment. Lay out your favorite, most comfortable riding clothes. This way, you won't stress yourself searching for your lucky socks or special jersey tomorrow morning. Check the weather report carefully. You may even want to call the local bureau of the National Weather Service. If it may turn cold, carry a jacket under your seat and take tights. If precipitation seems likely, take a rain jacket, a thin cap (to go under your helmet for warmth and dryness) and wool or polypropylene socks. (They may not be your luckiest, but they keep you warm when wet.) If the experts predict sun, bring tinted eyewear and sunscreen.

Nutrition. This dinner is important. Choose a bland, familiar, high-carbohydrate dish, such as spaghetti. Avoid spicy or fatty foods, plus anything that could cause indigestion or diarrhea. Also avoid alcohol and caffeine. Both are diuretics that decrease the amount of fluid in the body. Drink several glasses of water with and after the meal.

The Day

Training. Even if you rarely stretch, do it today. While your legs will eventually warm up during the multihour ride, your upper body can become stiff from inaction. To avoid this, try a couple of upper-body stretches. Stand three or four feet from your bike, with one hand on the saddle and the other on the stem. With your feet planted, bend your upper body toward the bike and move your chin toward your chest until you feel tension. Hold for about 30 seconds. This stretch loosens the neck, upper arms, back and shoulders.

To focus specifically on the shoulders and upper back, interlace your fingers behind you, with palms up. Slowly straighten your arms by lowering your joined hands, then gently rotate your arms backward. You'll feel a stretch in your shoulders. Hold it about 15 seconds. Repeat each of these stretches a few times before riding, at rest stops and after the event to minimize soreness.

Equipment. After you unload the bike from your car, double-check the tightness of the quick-releases. Spin the wheels to make sure a brake pad isn't rubbing. Take a short spin to check shifting (try low gear). Fully inflate your tires to decrease rolling resistance and prevent pinch flats, and don't forget your frame pump.

Nutrition. Limit your breakfast to 800 calories or less. To ensure complete digestion, give yourself one hour before the ride for each 200 calories you eat. For example, a large 800-calorie meal (five pancakes with syrup, orange, muffin, coffee) should ideally be eaten four hours before the start. A smaller, 200-calorie breakfast (a bowl of cereal or a bagel and juice) can be eaten within an hour of riding.

Drink several glasses of water with this meal, and another 15 ounces about 20 minutes before beginning. From the first five miles, drink either water or an energy drink, or both. Never go more than five miles without a gulp from your bottle. Nibble on food throughout. Avoid pigging out at the rest stops because having to digest large amounts of food diverts blood from your working muscles and could cause nausea.

Afterward, drink at least two glasses of water and have a huge, guilt-free, high-carbohydrate dinner to restock your muscles. Your test is over—and you passed. Let the celebrating begin.

9 THE DOUBLE CENTURY

As with so many other sports, one of the biggest thrills of cycling comes when you reach a kind of personal Holy Grail— something elusive or insurmountable suddenly becomes not only doable but done. When you first started cycling, going 20 miles was probably quite a challenge. But now you're starting to think about going ten times that distance!

If you can ride 100 miles relatively briskly and comfortably, you've reached the point where it's not unrealistic to consider doing a double century—200 miles in one day.

A "double" is more than two 100-milers back-to-back, however. It's a one-of-a-kind event that requires a different strategy and more careful preparation. Fatigue is a major factor, and proper nutrition is crucial. Conditions vary more, too. You may start in sunshine and finish 15 hours later in darkness and rain. You'll find parts of the ride painful and fight the temptation to quit. You'll probably knock back 20 bottles of liquid and consume 6,000 calories or more. But you'll also have the satisfaction of extending the limits of your mind and body and joining a select group of cyclists who have "done a double."

For advice on this advanced endurance event, we turn to Chris Kostman, a veteran of Race Across America (RAAM) and participant in the toughest double of all, the 200-mile Iditasport, ridden on mountain bikes over Alaska's snow-packed Iditarod dogsled trail.

How *Not* to Tackle This Event

My first double century, completed when I was 16, typifies the problems that can arise. I'd ridden eight centuries before this, with a best time of five hours, 45 minutes. I reasoned I could double the distance without any problem.

In preparation I logged as many miles as possible, often riding at dawn to get in 50 miles before school started. I did a few centuries and several races. During the final week I tried to eat well and get plenty of sleep.

I arrived at the start at 5:00 A.M., only to see all the participants departing into the darkness. I hurried to the registration table, but was told that because I had no lights, I couldn't start until sunrise. Someone offered me a small, battery-powered light and I was off, pushing a big gear in order to catch the pack.

Eventually I settled into a moderate pace and joined a group of riders for company and a break from the wind. It was a good move. With their help I covered the first 100 miles quickly, arriving at the turnaround in about seven hours. There, I stopped for 30 minutes—my first significant break.

Once I was back on the road, I discovered my muscles were painfully tight. I joined another paceline to help pass the miles. After several hours I could no longer stay with them. As the sun set, it began to get cold, and my light wasn't bright enough to even read the map. I cycled alone in the darkness. My knees began to hurt from having pushed too hard earlier in the day. I was underlit, underdressed and underfed. I crossed the finish line in 14 hours—a moment I'll never forget.

Since that day I've done numerous double centuries, as well as triple and quadruple centuries. My passion for distance led me to two Race Across America qualifiers (700 and 550 miles, respectively), and in 1987 I completed RAAM (3,129 miles) in ten days, 23 hours and 58 minutes. At age 20, I was the youngest rider ever to finish the race.

To this day I still use double centuries to gauge my fitness. Since that difficult and rewarding first double, I've lowered my time to 9:17. It took years of training, racing and experimentation to enable me to cover 200 miles so quickly and efficiently. Here are some of the things I learned.

Conditioning Is Vital

A double century requires long hours in the saddle, so it's important to be comfortable on your bike and have an efficient pedaling style. Consult with a bike shop that uses the Fit Kit or a similar bicycle sizing system to ensure that your riding position is correct and your cleats are properly adjusted. If changes are required, give yourself time to adapt.

As you train, concentrate on form. Maintain a brisk cadence (90 to 100 pedal revolutions per minute). If possible, have an experienced rider critique your pedaling style, or videotape yourself. You should pedal in smooth circles, and your knees should move vertically in one plane. Riding rollers is an excellent way to improve form.

Ride at least five days each week, gradually increasing intensity and mileage. Keep a training log, noting distance, time, average speed and terrain. Also record what you eat, how you feel, weight and resting heart rate. The latter (taken before rising each morning) is an excellent fitness indicator that can alert you to overtraining. When I'm stressed or at my lowest fitness level my heart zooms along at 55 beats per minute. When I'm at peak fitness it dips to 38 or lower. Heart rates are highly individual, though, so only by recording yours over time can you establish a meaningful pattern.

Your weekly program should vary in terrain and distance. Few double centuries are flat, so include one or two days of climbing. Do a fast-paced club ride once a week to increase speed and improve group riding skills. Maintain this program for at least six weeks.

A basic weekly schedule might go like this:

Saturday and Sunday: Long, high-intensity rides, 60 to 80 miles per day.

Monday: Easy spin, 15 to 25 miles.

Tuesday: Rest.

Wednesday through Friday: Gradually increase mileage and intensity, 30 to 60 miles per day.

For variety, try off-road riding, road racing or a triathlon. This is important, because if training gets boring it will also get less intense and less frequent. Crosstraining also enhances overall fitness, which is vital to fighting fatigue in long events. My weekly schedule often includes running, hiking, weightlifting, tae kwon do, racquetball and Ultimate Frisbee. I'm convinced these activities help my riding. Stretching also helps fight fatigue and prevents cramping.

But an athlete's body also needs rest, so do nothing strenuous at least one day each week.

Throughout your preparation, keep your goal in mind and visualize yourself achieving it. Cycling performance is 50 percent mental. It's determination that will see you through your training and enable you to cross the finish line.

Test Yourself (and Your Bike)

Gauge your fitness as the day of the double approaches. Try to comfortably complete a ride of about 125 miles, or ride back-to-back centuries one weekend. Ideally, you should do this with two weeks to go. Your time in this test will give you a rough idea of how to pace yourself in the double century.

You're not likely to improve much in the last few days, so don't overdo it in training. Also, now is the time to make sure your bike is working properly. It would be unfortunate not to finish because of a mechanical problem, so have questionable parts replaced.

Nutrition is vital during the last week. Load up on carbohydrates and fluids. I drink a gallon of water on each of these crucial days. Try to get enough sleep, particularly two nights before the event.

Double Day: Be Prepared

Allow plenty of time to travel to the start and register (if possible, preregister). Stay in a hotel the night before if the event is far from home. Eat a small, simple breakfast, but avoid all food during the half hour before the start, as it may upset your stomach.

Leave yourself enough time to stretch and loosen up. I prefer not to ride too much beforehand for fear of colliding with another distracted rider. Instead, use the first few miles of the event as your warm-up. Finally, check your equipment to be sure you're fully prepared.

I recommend carrying a small tool kit, two spare tubes, a patch kit, a folding tire, two or three large water bottles, emergency food such as an energy bar (in case you "bonk"), a cyclecomputer or watch, sun block and medical supplies, identification, money and a route sheet. If you anticipate riding in darkness, carry a high-quality cycling light. Your clothing should include a helmet, sunglasses, arm and leg warmers, windbreaker and gloves.

Some events are mass-start, while others allow you to leave when you please. In a mass-start don't bother trying to get to the front. It's too congested and dangerous. Be careful when the riders roll out—accidents often occur here.

During the first ten miles, stay off the large chainring. Once you're warm, try joining a paceline of smooth, safe riders traveling at a speed that doesn't make you labor. This will help you go faster, as well as provide good company. Don't overlap wheels with other riders, and stay away from those who seem unsteady. Eventually you'll find a group that suits you.

Eat and Drink Enough

As the miles pass, the important things to keep in mind are nutrition, hydration, comfort and pace. Try to consume 300 calories per hour. (A piece of fruit, for example, has roughly 100 calories. A bran muffin has about 150.) *Always* remember that you should drink before you're thirsty and eat before you're hungry.

Many riders consume a combination of fruit, cookies, muffins and granola bars. Keeping your energy stores high with these foods requires a lot of eating, however. You may also find your energy level varies considerably on such a sugary diet. To avoid these problems I use commercially available carbohydrate drinks. They're a well-balanced source of energy that the body can utilize quickly. If you choose a 100 percent liquid diet, it's imperative that you have experience with it prior to the event to avoid possible digestive problems.

Hydration is another vital component in maintaining energy. I drink one bottle of water per hour in addition to my liquid food. This is a lot of fluid, but it's necessary. (And in my opinion, other drinks should not be substituted for plain water.)

Try to Relax

Staying comfortable during a double involves many factors. Keep spinning a moderate gear. Get out of the saddle frequently to stretch your back. When you do stand, shift to a higher gear to maintain your speed. Well-padded gloves are helpful in fighting numbness, as is changing hand positions frequently. Shoes with hook-and-loop closures allow you to alter the pressure on your feet while riding. Insoles or orthotics help avoid foot fatigue. Wear comfortable, well-padded shorts. You might also benefit from a gel-type saddle.

During the ride use efficient pacing. Ideally, a double should not consist of one five-hour and one seven-hour century, but two six-hour centuries. Don't ride in a paceline that is beyond your ability, and pay attention to your current and average speeds. Use your rest time to eat, wash and stretch, and don't overeat. After finishing, have a good meal, drink plenty of fluids, and stretch to reduce soreness.

And if a 200-miler becomes as easy as a century, who knows? Maybe you even have what it takes to ride a RAAM someday.

10 HOW TO GUARANTEE A GREAT RIDE

Golfers forever treasure the scorecard of their finest round. Runners never forget a personal best. And cyclists always remember the ride of their life. Ask Bill Lang, who has ridden at least 100 miles

a day more than 700 times in the last decade. Which ride
was his favorite?

"I took a tour around Lake Michigan in '85," he quickly
recalls. "Had a tailwind the whole way, and the people were
incredible. Had a great time." Even six years (and tens of
thousands of miles) later, you get the idea he still remem-
bers the exact temperature, the jerseys he wore and what
he had for breakfast each day.

You can probably vividly remember your best ride,
too. Maybe it was the incredible scenery, the fulfillment of
a goal or just a day when you felt like—and, for once, rode
like—LeMond. Or maybe it's still to come.

If you've trained properly, you can make it happen. As
you approach the long-distance event you've been prepar-
ing for all season, whether it be a fall century or a tour,
maximize your odds with these 11 steps. They come from
century riders such as Lang, top road racers, members of
Bicycling's fitness advisory board and other successful cyclists.

When we canvased this diverse group looking for last-
minute preparation secrets and on-bike advice, we found
uncanny consistency to their answers. To them, these ac-
tions aren't simply tips, but a recipe for success. Do most
of them and you'll have a good ride. Do them all and you'll
have one to remember.

Focus on the ride. This was the most common word
used by our panel of experts. Andy Pruitt, a Denver athletic
trainer, recalls his victory in the 1987 World Disabled
Championships in France: "I was rested, well fed and mentally focused." Tom Schuler, who won the U.S. Pro Championship the same year, lists "focus and mental preparation" (ahead of rest, nutrition and training) as the most
important factors in the final week before an event. Ultra-
marathoner Susan Notorangelo says that for her best ride,
a victory in the 1989 Race Across America, "My focus was
the strongest I ever felt." And her husband, ultramarathon
legend Lon Haldeman, says it was "our focus throughout
the ride" that made his 1987 tandem transcontinental record with Pete Penseyres the ride of his life.

As you prepare, don't think of your big ride as a challenge, but as an opportunity. Finally, you get a chance to

show the kind of cyclist you are. Look forward to it. Become obsessive about it. In the final days, think of yourself as a thoroughbred—one dimensional, powerful and with blinders on.

Rehearse the event. A few weeks before the ride, do a dry run at the same time of day as the event and on the same course or a similar one. You don't need to complete the entire distance, but do at least 75 percent and ride at the pace you want to maintain on the big day.

Cycling physiologist Ed Burke considers such a rehearsal invaluable for preparation. Knowing you can handle the effort will increase your confidence. In addition, it lets you identify and solve problems, such as going out too fast in the early miles or eating or drinking too much or too little. It's also a good idea to drive the route, or at least the most difficult sections, so you aren't surprised by any steep climbs or dangerous corners.

Taper your training. "No training attempted in the last week will positively affect your event," says Pruitt. "It's only the training done the months before that will help."

During the last week, stay loose with some easy efforts. In the days before a century, 15 to 30 miles at an easy pace is plenty, and staying off the bike altogether is okay. This lets your body stockpile fuel and prepares your muscles for the major effort ahead.

When Pruitt flew to Europe for his championship ride, he got an unplanned layoff, courtesy of the airline, which had temporarily lost his bike. It arrived in time for the race, and Pruitt credits the rest for his sharpness.

Some cyclists, antsy from inactivity, go for runs or power walks and ruin their taper. Pruitt suggests staying off your feet as much as possible during the last week. It may seem like you're babying yourself, but doing so could be the small edge that leads to a great result.

If you need to combat the sluggishness of sitting around, David Smith, a doctor and cyclist, recommends "activities that don't involve much leg work, such as swimming." In any case, no matter what you do, don't do much of it.

Pack early. Stress saps energy, and few things are more taxing than searching for your pump, tights or jacket the morning of a major ride. The cyclists we interviewed say they ready their clothes and equipment (including provisions for all types of weather) at least a day beforehand. If it's an out-of-town event, it helps to pack the car early, too. It's a small concern, but the feeling that everything is taken care of reduces anxiety and boosts confidence.

Fill your tank. To ensure that your storage of glycogen is brimming, raise your carbohydrate intake as the ride approaches. Normally, 60 to 70 percent of your diet should be carbo calories. By the eve of the ride, increase this ratio to 90 percent. Eliminate fatty fare such as mayonnaise, fried foods, whole dairy products and creamy dressings and sauces.

On the day before your big ride, consume more water than on any other day of the year. Avoid alcohol, which negatively affects performance for 36 hours. Not only does it disrupt your iron balance and other elements, but by increasing urination it causes fluid loss, dooming your chances for peak performance.

Rest assured. You don't need a good night's sleep to have a great ride. In one study, even 60 hours of sleep deprivation didn't hinder subjects' strength or aerobic ability. So if preride excitement has you lying awake, don't fret. You can still do well.

"I've done a two-day, 200-mile ride with a minimum of sleep and had no repercussions," says Theresa Olsen, a cyclist from Springfield, Oregon, "because I was dedicated to the proper training in the months before."

During the last week simply strive to maintain your regular sleeping pattern. For an out-of-town ride, stay at a motel. It'll help you not only rest but also eliminate the anxiety and fatigue of a long morning drive.

Remember why you came. During the ride, make sure your mind doesn't wander too far from the opportunity at hand. You'll only get one chance to perform well so don't blow it with a lax attitude.

"Have a sense of purpose for the event," says Pruitt. "Know why you're doing it and what your goals are."

During a major ride, some cyclists review their goals and motivation at the start of every hour. It's a way of rededicating yourself and staying psyched. As Lang says about cycling success, if the preparation is right "it's all mental."

New York cyclist Richard Rosenthal discovered this in Switzerland on his first tour. Too petrified to climb a mountain pass, he changed his route and took a train to Italy. When he encountered formidable climbs there, he realized this was a demon he had to exorcise. He then returned to Switzerland, where he cleared the pass with ease. Since then, he's ridden the Alps many times and conquered other mountains, but he still considers that first experience the ride of his life. "All the difficulty had been in my head," he says.

Mind power takes many forms. For instance, Pruitt, infuriated by the airline losing his bike, put his anger into his pedal stroke and won. Others have exceeded expectations through the power of envy, frustration or love. Wherever it comes from, a mental edge is a valuable tool. Use it.

Buddy up. Many of the cyclists on our panel consider companionship a key factor. "Don't try to do it alone," says Lang. "The other person will keep you from quitting. You won't be able to dwell on your doubts or discomfort."

Not only that, but you can use your partner for drafting. One study shows that riding behind a person reduces your workload 1 percent for each mph of speed.

Keep pace. In the early miles of a big event, many cyclists ride too fast and consume valuable energy. "I try to remember that there's more to a century than the first 50 miles," says Oregon cyclist Monte Olsen.

The best approach is to ride consistently for the entire event, using a cyclecomputer to make sure you're at the right tempo.

"If your goal is a six-hour century, keep your speed between 16 and 17 mph," says Smith. "Pacing produces the maximum conservation of glycogen."

You can even divide your goal into ten-mile increments. For instance, to finish in six hours, each ten miles should take 36 minutes. Stay in this general zone, and you'll have no trouble reaching, or even exceeding, your goal.

Refuel. Between two and four hours before the ride, ingest 500 to 800 carbo calories and several glasses of water. Once it begins, gulp an energy drink or water at least every 15 minutes. Snack on energy bars or other high-carbo treats throughout, especially if you're drinking only water. This steady consumption is easier to digest than one large intake, which can interfere with muscle function.

Be lucky. To have the ride of your life, fate must be your stoker. Remember, even Lang, he of the 700 centuries, gave credit to that 1985 tailwind. Like the cliché says, luck is when preparation meets opportunity. So be prepared. It just might be your lucky day.

11 SLUMP BUSTING

Funny things happen to cylists around August. First, the highway department sneaks out at night and repaves all your favorite routes, adding 2 percent grade to each climb. Next, those tricky late-summer breezes roll in, so there's a headwind no matter which direction you pedal. Then your tires start slowly deflating during rides, but they're back to full pressure when you get home.

If you didn't know better, you'd think you were slowing down. But that can't be. You're at the peak of fitness. You've been training for months. The weather is perfect. You should be flying.

But you're not, and for once the highway department isn't at fault. The problem is burnout. You feel like you should be punching a time clock when you get on the bike. Your chainrings have turned to rectangles, and your legs don't want to turn at all. You're in a slump, mentally and physically.

It happens to the best of us. In fact, it only happens to the best of us. Burnout is a disease of overachievers, cyclists who never stop trying to go farther. Take a few days off? They'd rather be caught riding in black knee socks on a department store bike. Go for a spin with a slower friend? Not before you can pry their cold, stiff fingers from their brake hoods.

If you don't want to get fitted for a Lycra straitjacket, you have to learn how to overcome these training plateaus. And what better teachers than folks who stay (relatively) sane even though their cyclecomputers record more miles than your car's odometer? To find these Ph.D.'s of pedaling, we turned to that college of long-distance knowledge known as the Ultra-Marathon Cycling Association, whose members' idea of fun is doing consecutive double centuries.

These mileage junkies haven't discovered how to banish burnout, but all that time in the saddle has shown them ways to improve upon traditional slump-busting methods. Here are some of their secrets, along with the conventional wisdom they've refined.

Conventional wisdom: Take some time off.

Ultra wisdom: Build rest into your daily and yearly schedule.

Rick Stark of Lawndale, California (17,380 miles in 1990), takes every January off. "Even though I love to ride, I enjoy knowing the time will come each year when I can get off the bike," he says.

Adds Terry Wilson of Indianapolis (26,200 miles), "I'm a firm believer in one day off a week."

Conventional wisdom: Set goals.

Ultra wisdom: Set goals, but be flexible—and forgiving.

"Don't ever look at a failure [to meet a goal] as something bad," says Elaine Payne of Anaheim, California (10,000-plus miles). "Failure isn't really failure. You always learn something from your mistakes."

Adds Stark, "Some people are not in control of their cycling. The cycling is in control of them. You get to a point where you say, 'Oh my God, I'm a motor for my bicycle. I'm no longer a person.' "

Conventional wisdom: Ride different routes.

Ultra wisdom: Do everything differently.

"Mix up your ride with other complications," suggests John Lee Ellis of Charlotte, North Carolina (28,200 miles). "It forces you to think." Ellis meets other cyclists in the middle of his long rides, pedals to events such as club picnics or drives to new starting points. He suggests buying new gloves or handlebar tape "so you have something different to look at."

Conventional wisdom: Push yourself.

Ultra wisdom: Peak, taper and peak again.

"You have to do more than just ride the bike," says John Marino, UMCA president and former transcontinental record holder. "You have to scientifically ride the bike."

Ellis recommends analyzing your riding style by comparing it with that of classy co-riders and constantly tracking your fluid intake, pace, food requirements and other variables to determine what works best. "The more miles you put in of the same type, the harder it is to have an open mind," he says.

Stark gradually builds toward two peaks a year (June and October) instead of trying to maintain optimum fitness all season. He experimented with peaking three times a year but found that his high points weren't as lofty. "People who don't set up a schedule—who just ride hard—find they get into slumps that last," he says.

Conventional wisdom: Try a different kind of riding.

Ultra wisdom: Use every aspect of cycling to keep things fresh.

Stark rides a tandem ("ideal for fun," he says), goes touring ("traveling as opposed to training") or spins leisurely along the local bikepath ("sightseeing").

Susan France of Newberg, Oregon (12,000 miles), rides a mountain bike and helps organize cycling events in order to give others the kind of support and encouragement she's benefited from. "It's still cycling, but it's a fresh approach," she says.

Wilson rides occasionally with his wife, a casual cyclist.

And Ellis focuses on a big event, such as the 750-mile Boston-Montreal-Boston ride. "It puts the previous month in a whole different light because you're building to the event," he explains. "Talk about getting out of a rut. It's great."

12 THE FRESHNESS FACTOR

Sometimes when help arrives, we don't recognize it. Consider the case of pro road racer Davis Phinney. One spring, while riding beside the team car, his tires slipped on wet pavement and sent his bike underneath, where it was crumpled like a sheet of paper. Phinney, not wishing to inspect the muffler just then, tumbled in the other direction, suffering knee and back injuries. In the ensuing days, his aches and pains were so bad that he had trouble changing his son's diapers, much less going for four-hour training rides.

Normally, this would not be counted among the most fortuitous of events. Yet for Phinney, it was divine intervention. The crash altered his training with the authority that no coach could have mustered. It said: Time to rest.

Like any high-level athlete suddenly forced to run on idle, he began to fret. But when his injuries healed, he discovered he was flying. He rode strongly at a race in Arizona, then went on to win a stage and the sprinter's jersey at the Tour Du Pont. Next, he became the U.S. professional champion.

"I took two weeks off, missed some races and thought I would be useless," he reflects. "But in fact, for whatever reason, I felt great."

This episode, and others like it, caused Phinney to reevaluate his training. "Now I'm doing about 60 percent of the mileage I did in the past," Phinney says. "I used to do 500 to 1,000 miles per week. Now I'm doing 250 to 500, max. I'm taking more days off now than in the last five years combined.

"You can get so much in the mode of riding, riding. But I'm learning that you don't have to hammer yourself day in and day out to prepare for something. I'm trying to be completely fresh for specific goals."

Welcome to the new, kinder, gentler world of high-performance training. Phinney counts himself among the converted. So does Skip Hamilton, a successful ultra-distance runner and cross-country skier who serves as technical coach for a mountain bike team.

"There's been a definite shift toward decreased volume and higher quality with more rest," says Hamilton. "The most fundamental principle of improved performance is training with the appropriate amount of recovery. It's the most elusive part of a conditioning program, and it's the Achilles' heel of modern-day athletes."

Phinney's anecdotal evidence is grounded in science. David Costill, Ph.D., director of the Human Performance Lab at Ball State University, in Bloomington, Indiana, has conducted numerous studies of endurance athletes, including cyclists. His research with swimmers has shown that speed and power can increase after a two- to seven-week period of severely reduced training. Conversely, speed decreased in those on a high-volume program. In runners, increasing training from 50 to 60 miles per week to as much as 200 had no beneficial effect. "Hard training can cause a loss in power output and resting allows you to gain it back," says Dr. Costill. "Swimmers are convinced of this, but not athletes in other sports."

So all we have to do is sip Mai Tai's in the chaise lounge and reap the benefits, right? Unfortunately, no. Achieving quality rest can be as hard as completing a century ride in the mountains.

The problem is our infatuation with schedules. Long ago, someone decreed that we should rest on Monday, do hard training on Tuesday and Thursday and complete a long ride on Sunday. Fatigue, general malaise and overtime at the office be damned. However, this new approach to training asks that, heaven forbid, you become flexible.

"Now I wait for my body to feel good again after an event," says Phinney, 32. "I don't have a schedule that says one day I do this and one day I do that. After all these years, I'm getting sensitive enough that if I feel good, I know it. If I don't, I back off. It's worked wonders on my results. Before the pro championship there were five days when I didn't ride more than two hours. I just waited and waited for my body to feel good again."

Naturally, the flip side of the freshness factor is that you should train as hard as you rest. In fact, most riders find that they can ride at a higher level when they're sufficiently recovered.

So how do you know when you're in need of rest? Here are some cues.

Heart rate response with exercise. Exercise physiologists measure exertion with such exotica as expired gases, lactate levels and such. But for regular folks like us, there's heart rate. Elite athletes are intimately familiar with how high it gets, how long it takes to come down and what level can be maintained for various periods. You should be, too. Obtain a wireless monitor and use it as often as possible. "Often our perception of how we feel is not a true indication of our condition," says Hamilton. "A heart rate monitor separates these."

Warning signs include an inability to obtain a normal training heart rate, excessive recovery time (after climbs, for instance) or a heart rate that skyrockets with minimal effort. All these indicate that you should downgrade or eliminate that day's workout.

Resting heart rate. When your body is stressed, it works overtime to recover, even when you're sitting. This is reflected in your heart rate. Take your pulse under the same conditions each day, usually before rising. Once you know a baseline figure—say, 50 beats per minute—beware of increases of 10 beats or more. When this occurs, chances are you've done something violent (but hopefully productive) to your body. Consider it a sign that you should ride easy that day, or not at all.

Sleep. Hamilton recommends monitoring the quality of your sleep, not just the quantity. "Some athletes find they're always waking up in the night, sometimes with an accelerated heart rate. When you're recovered you should sleep restfully." Phinney has experienced both ends of the spectrum. "Sometimes I'm really tired and lethargic," he notes, "and at others I'm keyed up and can't sleep. I basically get out of touch with my body."

Energy on the bike. "When I'm rested I feel light on my bike," says Phinney. "I've got snap. On my way out of town on a training ride, I just pop over the hills." Hamilton says that you'll know within the first 20 minutes if you're up to an arduous workout. "Your metabolic and ventilatory systems are going as good as they're going to go by then," he says. "You can't do a quality workout when you're feeling tired. It's a mistake to think that if you push through, you'll get better."

Mood. "Connie says that when I lose my sense of humor, I need rest," says Phinney of his wife and training adviser. "I gnash my teeth over having to go riding." So beware if your home life suddenly degenerates into an episode from "The Simpsons." You may also find yourself cursing such routine impediments as cars, headwinds and potholes. Hamilton sees another red flag in the inability to do routine tasks such as paying bills and returning phone calls. "Excuses begin to take the place of daily responsibilities," he says. "You become a different personality."

Once you've established that you need rest, how should you take it? Cycling coaches have long advocated "bike walks" of an hour or so in which you put only light pressure on the pedals. But this may not be the best approach. Hamilton says that such active rest "satisfies our exercise addiction, but in reality you reach a point where you need time off. Otherwise, the bike becomes an object of a love/hate relationship.

"Do some other exercise. Go for a walk. It won't diminish your conditioning at all, and it will do wonders for your freshness."

13 BEATING FATIGUE

As mileage mounts on any ride, the door opens wider for that deep-down weariness we call fatigue. This is a constant threat to long-distance cyclists, so it helps to recognize the various symptoms and know the solutions. In fact, you'll see that it's relatively simple to fend off (or at least postpone) most factors that combine to cause fatigue. The result will be the ability to ride longer and stronger than ever before.

Fatigue affects almost every part of the body; knowing how to deal with it will greatly improve performance.

1. The Brain Plays Tricks

Causes and symptoms: During a long ride, your muscles deplete their supply of carbohydrate energy and trigger the release of an amino acid called tryptophan into the brain. This substance influences your mood. Meanwhile, intangibles such as anxiety and a lack of confidence or concentration can also flood your psyche. Sensing danger from all these developments, your brain tries to convince the body to slow down. One way it does this is by altering your perception. Suddenly, the effort seems harder than it is. The result is that even though your body may not be out of energy, your state of mind causes a sense of fatigue.

Solutions: There's nothing you can do about tryptophan entering your brain. But there are plenty of ways to keep your perceptions from becoming negative. Some guys do it by letting their minds wander. They think about hobbies, home, Cindy Crawford—anything but bikes. Another common abstraction is to imagine yourself in the Tour de France or Race Across America. Others find strength in total concentration, pondering the lead wheel in a paceline or counting each pedal stroke on a steep hill. Or you might mentally break the ride into several smaller sections, each offering a sense of accomplishment to move you toward the final goal—home. Experiment with these mind games. As long as you don't become oblivious to the road, any of them can positively affect your perceptions of a ride and lessen fatigue.

2. Neck and Shoulders Stiffen

Causes and symptoms: While your leg muscles deal with the fatigue caused by action, your shoulder and neck muscles have to handle the strain of inaction. For long periods, your neck must support the weight of your head and helmet, while your shoulders have to cope with the accumulating tension of a basically static riding position. Since there's little movement in the area, the muscles' only response is to contract and remain that way. This is the stiffening you feel on long rides.

Solutions: To reduce muscle tension and stiffness, try to avoid hunching your shoulders, especially when climbing. On flat, untrafficked sections of road, stretch your muscles. Loosen the upper body by periodically reaching behind you with one arm as if to receive a baton in a relay race. To keep your neck from getting stiff, wear a lightweight helmet and periodically roll your head from side to side.

3. Breathing Patterns Change

Causes and symptoms: You inhale air into your lungs, which deliver the oxygen via the bloodstream to your working muscles. As you pedal harder you take more breaths, and each one contains more air. But here's the catch: You may actually hold your breath at certain times during a ride, thus undermining this crucial system. It happens unconsciously, often from a lack of concentration or too much concentration. (Experts say it's natural to hold your breath when you must pay extreme attention, such as riding in a tight paceline or making a hairy turn.) Then when you do breathe, you must almost hyperventilate to compensate for the gap in oxygen intake. This odd breathing pattern is inefficient and fatiguing.

Solutions: Concentrate on taking deep, rhythmical breaths rather than shallow, quick ones. Always climb in an upright position so your lungs can fully expand. And most important, make sure your bike fits properly. Being doubled over a too-small frame or stretched out on one that's too big reduces your lung capacity.

4. Heart Hits Peak Level

Causes and symptoms: When you're riding, your heart pumps more blood, more often. Even if you're riding at only half your maximal intensity, the amount of blood your heart pumps is 50 percent more than at rest. Since the working muscles need extra oxygen and nutrients, this coronary blood flow is crucial. The more blood your heart can pump, the more efficient a cyclist you can be. Some hearts are efficient pumps, trained to work at a high percentage of their maximum. Others, however, simply can't move the blood fast enough, thus forcing an overall slowdown.

Solutions: Train. During two rides a week (nonconsecutive days), intersperse sprints with longer efforts of about five minutes, riding easily in between to recover. To extend your endurance, do at least one long ride per week. This is what aerobic fitness is all about: getting the maximum from your heart.

5. Back Hurts

Causes and symptoms: When cycling, your quadriceps aren't the only muscles at work. Your back is also in action, stabilizing your body and allowing the hips and legs to push forcefully. It's not an easy task. The cycling position puts an unusual strain on these muscles, especially if your bike doesn't fit properly. With the muscles in this tensed position for hours at a time, your back can stiffen. Once this central muscle group begins to bother you, it becomes difficult to continue at the same pace.

Solutions: Make sure your bike is sized to your particular dimensions. On a well-fitted road model, you should have a flat back while riding on the drops. (Check yourself with a stationary trainer and mirror, or when riding past a glass storefront.) A hunched back can occur if your handlebar is too high or your stem and top tube combination is too short. On a mountain bike, strive for a back angle of 45 degrees, which helps evenly distribute the workload among your butt, arms and legs. And vary your posture frequently during any ride.

6. Butt Aches

Causes and symptoms: When you push down on the pedals, much of the power comes from your gluteus maximus, the large buttocks muscle. To perform efficiently for thousands of pedal strokes, the glutes need energy and proper bike set-up. If either is lacking, early fatigue will result. Meanwhile, your rear-end tissue is also getting tired—tired of having a saddle wedged into it. This is manifested by a pain in the butt, which may be the overwhelming factor in causing new riders to limit the distances they ride or even stop cycling altogether.

Solutions: To maximize the use of your glutes, set your saddle high enough so that your knees bend slightly at the bottom of each pedal stroke. Then when riding, stand occasionally to stretch. And to solve the problem of tissue soreness, adopt a consistent riding schedule. The more time you spend in the saddle, the tougher your hind tissue gets. Women may find more comfort on one of the anatomic saddles made by several companies.

7. Glycogen Stores Run Out

Causes and symptoms: When you ride, you use 10 to 20 times as much energy as you do at rest. As your intensity rises, the muscles rely heavily on their premium fuel, glycogen (carbohydrate in its stored form). After about two hours of steady, fast riding with no carbohydrate intake, this fuel is exhausted. At this point, your muscles begin relying mostly on stored fat. But this is an inefficient energy source. In fact, while using it your body can sustain only 50 to 60 percent of its maximum aerobic capacity.

Solutions: Emphasize endurance training, which increases your ability to store glycogen. Well-trained muscles also become adept at using other fuels, thus saving the glycogen for late in a ride. So beef up your mileage at least two days each week. At the same time, build your diet around high-carbohydrate foods such as fruits, vegetables, pasta and breads. The week before a big event, increase carbo intake and decrease training to keep your glycogen stores brimming. During a long ride, ingest high-carbo foods and sports drinks.

8. Lactic Acid Accumulates

Causes and symptoms: When your muscles burn fuel during an intense effort such as a steep climb, the process produces a waste product called lactic acid. Studies show that even a 10-second sprint can bathe muscles in it. But although lactic acid has been heavily researched, it's still unknown exactly how it causes fatigue. What is known is this: The acidity interferes with the muscles' ability to turn food into energy. At the same time, it interacts with other substances in muscle and somehow contributes to fatigue. The acid also draws in water, which lowers blood volume. This makes it harder to deliver oxygen and impossible to sustain a hard effort for long.

Solutions: Keep your pace and effort below the level that produces a rush of lactic acid. Proper gearing and shifting technique are essential, especially when you're riding in the hills.

9. Electrical Power Declines

Causes and symptoms: The way your muscles work is wondrous. But like most wonders (a light bulb, for instance) there's a secret behind the magic. In the case of your muscles, it's the same as a light bulb's—electricity. For the muscle to work, there must be an electrical potential across the membrane of the muscle fiber. But there's a problem: The enzyme that allows the muscle to maintain its electrical properties is sensitive to temperature changes. And muscles at work create heat. The enzyme reacts negatively to this, causing the muscle to lose its electrical power and its energy to flicker out.

Solutions: None. This is one of the reasons that no cyclist, not even Greg LeMond, can escape the throes of fatigue.

10. Feet Swell

Causes and symptoms: In the late stages of a ride, your feet can feel hot and numb. This can stem from two sources. First, your shoes may become tight as your feet swell slightly, giving you what cyclists call "hot feet." This occurs when blood circulation is restricted at the ball of the foot or nerves are compressed, causing tingling and burning sensations. Second, your toe straps may be too tight, numbing the top of the foot and toes. In either case, the condition causes increasing discomfort and may even force you to stop.

Solutions: Wear cycling shoes that aren't too snug. The extra sole stiffness they offer is essential during long rides. Loosen the laces or strap fasteners at the first sign of discomfort. Also, keep your toe straps slightly loose. Except for sprints or climbs, it's not necessary to cinch them tight.

11. Exercise Poisons Build

Causes and symptoms: When you're riding for hours, a compound called monovalent phosphate tries to slow you. Studies suggest that this substance affects the structure of muscle tissue. Muscle fibers are connected by microscopic bridges that contract to produce work. The monovalent phosphate somehow interferes with the movement of these key bridges. As this substance accumulates, the muscle loses strength; as it declines, the muscle regains power. Two other bodily substances have the opposite effect. A compound called phosphocreatine and an enzyme known as ATP are abundant in working muscles but hard to find in fatigued ones. Within ten seconds after you stop riding, their quantities are restored to prior levels. While it's unknown how these substances work, many experts believe they are prime suspects in the mystery of fatigue.

Solutions: Only in the last two decades have scientists been able to discover some of the mechanisms that cause fatigue. However, they have yet to offer solutions to these performance-limiting problems.

12. Hands Go Numb

Causes and symptoms: As a ride progresses, your hands feel the toll. Gripping the handlebar puts pressure on the ulnar nerve, which runs through the palm. This can result in tingling and numbness which, in turn, can cause weakness or even loss of muscular control in your fingers.

Solutions: Use thick bar wrap and wear cycling gloves to provide padding and shock absorption. Also, maintain a relaxed grip whenever conditions permit, and periodically change from the drops to the bar tops to the hoods (as decribed in chapter 4). Flutter your fingers every few miles. On a mountain bike, avoid overly soft grips that make you squeeze too hard.

13. Arms Tire

Causes and symptoms: Every bump you ride over sends a shock wave into your bike and through your arms. This jars and tires the forearm muscles. At the same time, you're using your arms to subtly pull or push the handlebar as you complete each pedal stroke. When you're steering a mountain bike along a tight singletrack, the arm workout is especially energy-consuming. Though most of your attention may be on your legs, the fatigue in your arms contributes to overall exhaustion late in a ride.

Solutions: Set your saddle so it's level or pointed up slightly. This keeps you from sliding forward and having to resist it with your arms. Also, ride with your elbows loose and bent to absorb road shock. If it's impossible to do this comfortably, you probably need a shorter stem or top tube. To develop more strength and endurance in your arms, supplement your cycling with rowing or weight work in the off-season.

14. Muscles Overheat

Causes and symptoms: Your blood does more than deliver oxygen and nutrients to the working muscles. It also removes the heat they generate and carries it to the skin, where it's eliminated, primarily by sweating. During an intense ride, as much as half a gallon of perspiration can be lost every hour. This water comes directly from your bloodstream. (It's actually the blood's watery portion, known as plasma.) When plasma volume is reduced through sweating and no water is ingested, your blood can't effectively remove the heat and your temperature rises. This brings a throbbing head, chills and overall weakness. Since 45 percent of all body fluid is stored in muscles, the drop in plasma volume affects them hard, usually with cramps and fatigue.

Solutions: To maintain your plasma volume, you need fluid. Water is okay, but studies show that it can be more effective when it's in a carbohydrate-rich sports drink, which provides fuel as well as fluid. During a ride, drink early and often.

15. Water Levels Drop

Causes and symptoms: Your body is 60 percent fluid. In fact, most of the internal metabolic energy production that's essential for exercise takes place in water. This is one reason why maintaining an optimum body fluid level is so important. Studies show a deficit of just 4 percent can reduce aerobic work capacity by almost 50 percent. As you ride, your fluid level steadily declines because of sweating and muscle use. If not replaced, this can lead to dehydration. Symptoms include dry mouth, lack of sweat, chills and severe fatigue.

Solutions: Drink a glass of water before riding, then keep drinking water or a sports drink on the bike. Don't go longer than 10 to 15 minutes without sipping some, and try to average about a bottle an hour, or more if it's hot. And never wait until you're thirsty to drink. Thirst is a poor indicator of your body's fluid needs.

16. Eyes Strain

Causes and symptoms: Sunshine and fresh air are two great reasons to ride, but they're also two main causes of eye fatigue. Invisible ultraviolet rays can overwhelm the eyes—even on cloudy days. Glare and bright light cause

squinting, which tires facial muscles and can cause head-
ache. And rushing air dries the lenses. In response, your
eyes water, which can cloud vision and make you feel tired.

Solutions: Wear shades. Several manufacturers make
high-quality sunglasses for cyclists, offering relief from ultraviolet rays, wind and fatiguing squints.

14 HOW TO RIDE THROUGH WINTER

Winter isn't a great time of year to be a cyclist. In many
parts of the country, the air is cold enough to turn your
bike into a superconductor, the roads are crusted with ice
and motivation levels have plummeted lower than the temperature. Even if you live in the Sunbelt, early darkness can
be just as frustrating as freezing temperatures.

By December, all the aerobic animals you trained with
in July have gone into hibernation. You've resigned yourself
to the resistance trainer, you've seen that Tour de France
video so often you've memorized the script and the first
club ride or tour seems centuries away. But even on winter's darkest, dreariest days, you can still ride outside.
What's more, if you're properly equipped and know a few
tricks, it doesn't have to be a heroic struggle. In fact, winter
riding is one of the sport's best-kept secrets.

Let's see how cyclists ride through winter in areas as
diverse as the snow-covered Rockies and sunny Arizona.
By joining them, you will not only enjoy the invigorating air
and exercise, but you will keep a higher percentage of the
endurance you worked all year to build, making you that
much stronger when the new season begins.

Take It Easy

The first rule for riding through winter is: Don't ride
through winter—at least not too hard.

Many avid cyclists have hammered away from Christmas to Easter, only to be physically exhausted and emotionally flat when the cycling fireworks go off in July. So winter riding should be low-key and interspersed with other activities.

Holly Rouillard, a fast-recreational rider from Denver, epitomizes the correct balance between cycling and winter sports. "I ski all winter to avoid burnout from trying to ride year-round," she says. "But I do ride a stationary bike and lift weights to maintain cycling fitness."

Jack Panek is president of the West Elk Road Club in Gunnison, Colorado, and often advises young riders. He tells them, "Give yourself a break early in the season. Don't be worried if you get dropped on club rides. You will peak later and be stronger than people who train hard in February and burn out in July."

It isn't just a matter of physical fatigue from a long season, either. Getting out the door when it's 20°F or rushing home to squeeze in a ride before it gets dark requires willpower and dedication that's better saved for April and May. One way to ensure automatic daily miles is to become a bike commuter, cycling to and from your job or classes each day. This is likely to require equipment for riding in the dark, however. (See page 86.)

If you live in the Sunbelt, don't be tempted to take advantage of those mild winters and train hard. Ralph Phillips, a rider from Tucson, has seen some terminal cases of overtraining, especially among northern cyclists who go to Arizona for winter riding.

"I encourage people to ease off in the winter so they don't burn out by midsummer," he says. National-caliber racer Leslee Schenk agrees: "Even in a warm climate, I think it's important to get off the bike to clear your head. It's fine to keep riding, but the pressure should be off. Go on a long ride with friends, and take a picnic lunch."

Dress Properly

While you don't want to overdo winter riding, you do want to maintain fitness for cycling. Indoor resistance trainers help, but even highly motivated cyclists can't crank away for long. There's just no substitute for moderate road miles.

Panek is probably the epitome of the hardcore winter rider. Living in Gunnison, a Colorado town that sits at 7,700 feet and annually vies for the dubious distinction of the coldest place in the country, he must sometimes contend with − 40°F temperatures. Despite such harsh winters, Gunnison produces some outstanding racers and has a surprisingly large core of fast-recreational riders. Panek has lived there for 20 years and knows all the winter riding tricks.

He protects himself from the cold by dressing in layers. "I like an inner layer of polypropylene or a similar synthetic fiber," he explains. "Over this I wear another polypro layer and then a wool jersey. On top I wear a waterproof shell that breathes, so perspiration doesn't build up. Dark colors absorb more sunlight."

Adequate ventilation is just as important as layering. If you overheat, sweat will soak the inner layers and you'll chill when the mercury drops or you turn into the wind. If the temperature rises during a ride, Panek sheds one or more layers, stowing them in his jersey pockets. If he encounters headwinds or snow squalls, he puts them back on. "Zippered turtlenecks are good for inner layers," he adds, "because you can zip or unzip them in response to temperature changes."

It takes only minor modifications to adapt this basic cold weather ensemble to extreme conditions. "When the temperature drops below freezing, you have to be really careful of knees, hands and feet," Panek says. "Tights with knee-warming inserts are great, and I often wear wool leg warmers under them for more protection. Sometimes I use old socks with the toes cut off and just pull them over the knee. Newspaper works well if you get cold on a ride and can find some lying around. Tear several layers about a foot square and put them against your chest.

"For the hands," he continues, "cross-country ski gloves work fine in cool weather but aren't enough protection when it's cold. Then I wear regular downhill gloves. Get them a size larger because you don't want tight gloves cutting off your circulation when your hands are gripping the brake levers."

Feet are usually the first thing to freeze. Neoprene or pile-lined, insulated shoe covers do the best job of keeping your tootsies toasty. Make sure the outer material is waterproof. Also, wool socks help hold body heat even if they become wet.

In moderate conditions, a lightweight ski hat under your helmet will keep your head warm. Take a few sizing pads out of the helmet for a more comfortable fit. But "some people have trouble with hats," Panek points out. "Around here we also use Swix earmuffs designed for cross-country skiing. They keep your ears warm, but your head won't overheat."

In very cold conditions, especially with a headwind, it's possible to get a frostbitten face. Panek recommends wearing a lightweight polypropylene or silk balaclava under your helmet. Goggles or sunglasses under the balaclava will keep its window from moving.

Male riders need to guard against penile frostbite, a particularly gruesome cold-weather riding hazard that can strike before you notice. Wear several layers and look for tights with a nylon wind panel in the appropriate area.

Be Flexible

In most sections of the country, winter doesn't attack in November and continue unabated until March. Instead, cold snaps are interspersed by more temperate days when riding can be pleasurable. Monty George lives and rides at 6,500 feet in Durango, Colorado, where two-foot snowfalls aren't uncommon. But neither are 60°F midwinter days. "Sometimes I can ride the mountain passes in February," he says. "It'll snow and the roads will be snowpacked for days, but then it will melt off. The trick is planning your schedule so you can ride when the weather is right."

By the same token, be prepared to ride outside in spurts during the winter. You may have several days or even weeks of good weather when you can get into a summer riding pattern. This is great, but you'll have to make the mental adjustment when the inevitable bad weather returns and you're back on the resistance trainer. To make the transition easier, consider midwinter riding as a bonus. This way, the grudging return to indoor training won't seem as hard. Also, don't plan a rigid training schedule that bad weather may disrupt. Be flexible. Says George: "Get up in the morning, see how the weather is and decide what to do that day for training."

With experience, you'll discover what temperatures you can tolerate. Because cold can irritate tendons, be careful if you have a history of injury. Panek, who has suffered severe Achilles tendinitis, explains there's a fine line between when you should and should not ride. "My cutoff temperature has gone up as I've gotten older," he says. "If you have a problem with tendinitis, err on the safe side."

Get Fat (Tires)

Even on near-zero days, runners can train outdoors in calm conditions with minimal clothing. This is because aerobic exercise generates tremendous body heat and running's slow speed produces negligible wind chill. However, if there's a 20-mph headwind, runners will freeze-dry in a hurry. This is why it's more difficult to cycle during the winter than run. Even on calm days the greater speed produces a wind chill that saps precious body heat. A cyclist riding 20 mph on a calm 20° day, for instance, is exposed to a wind chill factor of −10°F. (See the table on the opposite page.)

The solution? Emulate pro road racers such as Andy Hampsten, Steve Bauer and Phil Anderson, who ride mountain bikes on the road. They've learned that the fat, knobby tires and upright position slows you to the point where you minimize wind chill but still get a good workout. Maintaining the same heart rate, you can ride 20 mph on a road bike and get cold, or crank along at 12 or 13 mph on a mountain bike and remain comfortable. Panek notes another advantage: "The fat tires help you handle ice and snow on the road."

Calculating Wind Chill

Wind Speed (mph)*	Air Temperature (°F)							
	+50	+40	+30	+20	+10	0	−10	−20
5	48	37	27	16	6	−5	−15	−26
10	40	28	16	4	−9	−24	−33	−46
15	36	22	9	−5	−18	−32	−45	−58
20	32	18	4	−10	−25	−39	−53	−67
25	30	16	0	−15	−29	−44	−59	−74
30	28	13	−2	−18	−33	−48	−63	−79
35	27	11	−4	−20	−35	−51	−67	−82
40	26	10	−6	−21	−37	−53	−69	−85
	Little Danger				**Increasing Danger**			**Great Danger**

SOURCE: From "Inside the Cyclist," *Velo-News,* 1979.
*Identical to riding speed on a calm day. Otherwise, add or subtract wind speed to or from riding speed, depending on whether you are riding against the wind or with it.

Adds Schenk: "It's a great auxiliary way to train that simulates the road bike. You're still riding but it's different, so mentally you stay fresh." There's no need to limit yourself to the pavement, though. "Physically, it's hard plowing through the drifts or mud," says Schenk, "but it's great for power and bike handling. When I descend on my road bike, I'm more comfortable after descending on my mountain bike."

If you don't want to invest in a mountain bike, Panek suggests installing fat clinchers (700 × 32C) on your road bike.

Rearrange Routes to Avoid Hills and Wind

Another cold-weather riding tip is to avoid long hills. When climbing you'll stay warm due to the combination of reduced speed and hard work. But while descending you'll shiver even if you're wearing enough polypro and Gore-Tex to start a clothing store. Also, winding descents can hide dangerous icy patches in shady corners that could cause a crash. Conversely, short rolling hills are fine if the pavement is dry. They can even help you stay warm because the descents are brief enough so you'll retain the heat you produced on the climb.

Also, check the prevailing wind before leaving home. It's better to head into the wind during the first half of your ride. Then, if you get damp with perspiration from the effort, you will have the freezing wind at your back on the return leg. A tailwind hustles you home to a warm shower faster, too.

See and Be Seen after Dark

Like a boxer, winter hits cyclists with a one-two punch. If cold weather doesn't KO your training plans, early darkness will. Improved lighting and reflector systems make it possible to ride confidently at night, but depending on the traffic on your roads you still may not be as safe as in daylight. Plus, you'll have to festoon your bike and person with several pounds of safety equipment.

If you decide to do it, start with a good headlight to illuminate road hazards, as well as reflectors on the pedals and frame to make you visible to motorists. You can save weight and money by sticking long strips of reflective tape on an old bike's frame and crankarms. Don't try it on your good bike, though, because the stuff just doesn't peel off come spring. Another tip is to wear a reflective vest. Phillips also suggests "a caving-type light fixed to your helmet. Wherever you look, that's where the light points." As you can see, the idea is to look like a supernova so motorists can't help but notice. Think Broadway, and put your body and bike up in lights.

Whether to go with battery- or generator-powered lights is a basic question you'll face. Wet or icy conditions can make a generator slip on the tires, while batteries have reduced life in the cold. To remedy the latter problem, consider lights with rechargeable batteries. Most will keep you well lit for about three hours, then return to full power overnight.

Even if you work from 9 to 5, you can still get outside after daylight saving time expires without resorting to night riding. Phillips suggests two alternatives: "Some people here in Tucson ride during their lunch hour. Those who can't do indoor exercise all week and then ride on the weekend."

So, don't let bad weather make this your winter of discontent. Instead, mix weight training and aerobic activities with some no-pressure winter riding. When spring does come, you'll be fit and eager.

15 GETTING STRONGER, CYCLING LONGER

Until the 1980s, cyclists rarely lifted weights. In fact, weight training was spurned by most endurance athletes, and the physique of choice was the marathoning ideal— lean to the point of emaciation. Few cyclists had weight training experience, and most coaches didn't believe it could help riders improve. Iron was anathema.

But now, in one of training theory's periodic about-faces, everyone is pumping iron enthusiastically. What happened? On the recreational side, cyclists got tired of wimpy upper bodies. (It's no coincidence that the move to weight training coincided with the popularity of snug-fitting Lycra.) Vanity aside, the Eastern European countries demonstrated that with strength comes speed. The great East German and Soviet sprinters were built like Greek gods.

For long-distance riders, weight training came to be seen as a way to condition the upper body for the rigors of hours in the saddle. It was once thought that the best way to do this was simply to ride, and the arms, shoulders, neck and back would adapt. Now we realize that weights can effectively build the required strength, making the season's first long rides more comfortable and allowing endurance to improve at a faster rate.

Despite this new enthusiasm for weights, however, scientific findings from the National Strength and Conditioning Association indicate that many cyclists are going about it all wrong. Circuit training, high repetitions, endless squats—all have had their outspoken advocates. But here's what's really been learned about weight training and cycling.

Strength means aerobic power. We used to think that cyclists were aerobic athletes, shotputters were strength athletes, and never the twain should meet. Now we know that VO_2 max, the lab test that measures oxygen consumption and indicates cycling potential, is inseparable from leg strength. For proof, recall a day when your legs were tired from several consecutive hard rides and no matter how hard you tried, you couldn't elevate your heart rate. If you had taken a VO_2 max test, the results would have been far below your potential.

Now suppose your legs felt fresh but they lacked strength. You'd experience the same disheartening results. "If your legs are too weak to drive your heart and lungs to maximum levels, your max VO_2 performance will be low," explains David Martin, exercise physiology researcher at the Olympic Training Center in Colorado Springs. "Strengthen the legs and you can improve your peak VO_2 and your cycling performance."

Peter Francis, Ph.D., renowned for his work in cycling biomechanics, agrees with this basic change in training philosophy. "The traditional approach to cycling was to ride a great deal," he says. "Now we believe that cycling inefficiently only trains you to cycle inefficiently. We know that specific strength training is important."

Weight training prevents injury. This benefit is vital to competitors and to recreational riders who don't want the loss of fitness and health that accompanies downtime. Weight training strengthens the shoulder girdle and neck, helping it withstand overuse injuries and absorb crash trauma. A good leg program balances the strength of the opposing quadriceps and hamstrings, helping you avoid muscle pulls and tears from hard efforts. Weight training is your injury insurance policy.

Moderation is vital to improvement. Successful cyclists don't overdo iron therapy. "The difference between fitness and fatigue is performance," says Martin. If your legs are dead from too much strength work, you won't benefit from time on the bike.

Likewise, don't be afraid that you'll lose fitness as you rest. "Fatigue is eliminated faster than fitness," explains Martin. Also, there's no cycling-related reason to build bulging biceps, and a 400-pound deadlift is useful only in hoisting your bike onto the roof rack.

"Don't waste time in the weight room," stresses Harvey Newton, a masters racer and a former U.S. Olympic weightlifting coach. "Get in, do a cycling-specific strength workout, and then go on to something else." The late Carl Leusenkamp, a national team track coach, told his riders, "Don't let weight training become an end in itself. Use weights to help you go faster on the bike."

Plan for best results. Early attempts at incorporating weight training into cycling programs often failed because they were badly planned. Know what you want from strength training before you begin. Each fall, formulate your goals for the coming year. "Look at the end of the riding season as the beginning of your year," advised Leusenkamp. "Evaluate and plan." A valuable tool is a training diary, which helps you evaluate your performance and stay motivated.

Use periodization to structure workouts. Athletes in all sports vary their training to avoid staleness and create periods of peak performance. "You need a long-range, year-round approach to training," explains Newton, "because the road cyclist has only about four months to do serious strength training." He suggests starting in October with a transitional weight training phase lasting about four weeks. By varying the exercises, using light weights with higher repetitions and working out two or three times a week, you'll slowly accustom your muscles to lifting. Ease gradually from riding to weight training because, as Francis warns, "The best predictor of injury is change."

Next comes a four- to six-week "hypertrophy" or preliminary strength-building period. It features thrice weekly workouts using three or four sets of each exercise done for 8 to 12 repetitions apiece. Both of these early phases are vital. "If you begin strength training without transitional and hypertrophy periods," warns Newton, "you'll get injured."

Only then are you ready for the meat of the program—four to six weeks of basic strength development using five or more sets of each exercise with no more than 8 reps apiece. Conclude with a month of power development by doing three or four sets of exercises specific to cycling (leg presses, step-ups, lunges) using slightly higher reps (about 15) and greater speed of movement.

Don't let your hard-earned strength deteriorate during the riding season. Maintain it, says Newton, "with dips, pull-ups, abdominal work and neck exercises" twice a week. But don't forget that your priority is cycling. "When the road season begins, is not the time to set records in the weight room," says Newton.

Forget calf raises and circuit training. When planning your training, don't repeat the mistakes of the past. For example, calf raises have traditionally been part of cycling weight programs. After all, when you ride behind someone with impressive calves it looks as if they're vital to the pedal stroke. But according to Francis, "It's the quads that are actually flexing the foot. The calf muscles act merely as a tight wire to transfer the quads's power to the foot and pedal." So, forgo the calf exercises and focus on developing the quad power that really counts.

Circuit training has been similarly misinterpreted. Long a staple at U.S. Cycling Federation winter development camps, it involves a series of light-weight/high-repetition exercises to build muscle endurance and cardiovascular fitness. Research, however, now indicates that its effect on aerobic fitness is minimal. Because of this, Newton recommends using weights for their primary purpose—improving strength. "I recommend three to five sets of about ten reps rather than high-rep training or circuits," he says.

Do less to benefit more. There's no reason to spend hours in the weight room, even in midwinter. Six exercises packed into 30 minutes are all you need. Choose an exercise for the quads, an upper-body pulling movement such as bent-over rows, and a pushing exercise such as bench presses. (See accompanying illustrations.) Then add two "assistance" exercises such as abdominal crunches and back extensions. "Cyclists use lower back muscles to keep from straightening up on powerful pedal strokes," explains Francis. "They also need strong abdominals to avoid back injuries."

Vary the number of repetitions and the weight used for each exercise with the training period (hypertrophy, power, etc.). Come spring, you'll be an ironman on the bike.

Step-Up

Experts say this exercise is safer for the back and better for the quads. Begin with your thigh parallel to the floor ... and don't push off with your rear leg.

Bench Press

This exercise is important for arm muscles that support a cyclist's upper body.

Crunches

The key to protecting your back is strengthening your abs.

Leg Press

To build powerful quads, alternate leg presses with stationary cycling.

Row

This routine improves shoulder/arm strength as the bar is pulled to the chest and lowered slowly.

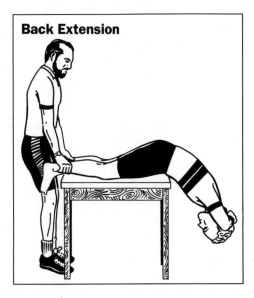

Back Extension

To build strength safely, don't rise above the horizontal.

Tips from a Top Coach

The Bulgarians have been at the forefront of strength development in recent years. Because their lifters have won Olympic and world titles disproportionate to their country's population, their coaches have become leaders in applying the principles of strength development to other sports. Extensive research and careful observation put their methods on the cutting edge of weight training theory. Bulgarian national weightlifting coach Angel Spassov offered some advice for cyclists during a recent U.S. lecture tour.

Be patient. Weight training is not a quick fix. Three weeks or three months in the weight room won't elevate you from a century rider to Paris-Brest-Paris champion. According to Spassov, "You need six to eight years of training to be world class in any sport." The body will improve but only on its timetable. Forcing rapid improvement in cycling or weight training leads to injury, stalled progress and staleness. "Always when we break the laws of nature," he says, "we make mistakes."

Use technology. The same heart rate monitor that's so valuable for training on the bike is also useful for winter weight workouts. In endurance sports, you elevate your heart rate to 150 to 180 bpm (depending on your age) during interval training and let it drop to about 120 for recovery. Nearly the same principles apply to strength training. "In power sports," explains Spassov, "strength is best built in the 160 to 180 range. But let your heart rate drop lower— 102 to 105—between sets."

Use weights to develop cycling-specific strength. Doing intervals up steep hills builds cycling power. But so do leg presses—and they do it faster. "It's hard to use your sport—cycling, rowing, etc.—to develop power to its fullest," says Spassov. "You need weights. You can use your sport but it takes much longer with aerobic sports."

For endurance cyclists, this supports the contention that upper-body strength can be developed better in the weight room than on the bike. Bench presses, rows, crunches and back extensions are particularly effective at conditioning the muscles likely to fatigue during long rides.

Endurance doesn't exist separately from strength. "Endurance isn't alone," says Spassov. "It's all strength." For example, he explains that a runner takes about 27,000 steps during a marathon and with each step pushes two times his or her body weight. That's about 1,600 tons over the 26 miles, so the need for strength is evident. In addition, Spassov maintains that while the marathon runner's heart rate returns to normal about three hours after the event and the blood profile is back at baseline in three days, the legs need about a month to recover. So the more strength the legs possess, the faster the recovery.

For endurance training, keep the resistance low to maintain speed and technique. Spassov recommends working with 28 percent of your one-rep maximum to build endurance. For instance, if you can bench press 150 pounds one time, do multiple reps with 40 pounds to build endurance.

Step up to step-ups. Traditional back squats have always been the cornerstone of strength programs, but they are no longer done in the Bulgarian system. "Squats put too much compression on the lower back," explains Spassov, "and there's no correlation between squat performance and sports performance." As a result, the Bulgarians have substituted a special version of that old reliable, step-ups (see page 91). Most authorities still advocate squats and maintain that they won't cause injury if done correctly. But if squats give you the back miseries, try the Bulgarian alternative. Some caveats include:

1. Choose a bench that's high enough so your thigh is parallel to the ground when you're on your toes with the rear leg.
2. Don't alternate legs after each rep. Instead, keep the right or left leg on the bench until you have done the planned number of reps, then switch legs. Also, don't push off with the rear leg. Staying on the toes of your rear leg will ensure that all the work is done with the bent leg.
3. Start the exercise using just your body weight as resistance. As you get stronger, hold a barbell or inner tube filled with sand over your shoulders— but don't use more than your maximum squat or leg press divided by 2.2.

Mix weight training and cycling. In the early season, Spassov recommends an easy warm-up of 15 minutes on the bike or stationary trainer followed by intervals of hard pedaling mixed with easy ones. Then get off the bike, change shoes and do a short, intense program of leg development—step-ups, leg presses and so forth. Back on the bike, spin easily for 15 minutes to cool down. Mixing cycling and weight training in the same workout ensures that the strength you're building transfers to the specific movement of cycling. You'll keep your pedaling finesse and get stronger.

Part Four
NUTRITION FOR THE LONG HAUL

16 EATING FOR ENDURANCE

Finally, the last rest stop. After ten hours and 175 miles of a hot and grueling double century, Ellen has reached the final break. Although she has some minor aches and pains, she doesn't feel too bad. She relaxes in the shade, eats a few chocolate chip cookies and ponders the nutritional strategy that's gotten her here.

Because Ellen is an exercise physiologist and registered dietitian, other riders expect her to be immune to exhaustion. That always gives her a chuckle, because there are no secrets to it. A basic understanding of what the body needs to perform efficiently during extended rides can allow any cyclist to perform better.

One key is eating. In fact, on any ride longer than three hours, you must eat and eat plenty. Here's why: A 150-pound person (for example) cycling at 15 mph burns about 500 calories per hour. This translates into 125 grams of carbohydrate, since each carbo gram has four calories. Studies show that you must replace about half this amount in order to keep riding efficiently. Thus, each hour you must eat the equivalent of one banana (105 calories) and half a bagel (80 calories), while taking several gulps (one cup) of a sports drink (50 to 70 calories).

This might sound like a lot, but your body requires it during long rides. Without such refueling, your energy stores will become exhausted.

It's not just how much you eat, though. What you consume is also important. For instance, fatty foods are not converted to energy quickly enough to fuel a hard ride. High-carbohydrate foods are. Here's how it works:

Carbohydrate is either stored in the muscles as muscle glycogen or directed toward the liver, which dumps it into the circulatory system as blood glucose. In the first two hours of exercise, your body relies mostly on existing glycogen stores for energy, so there's no need to eat during short rides. But on rides lasting two hours or more, you deplete the glycogen stores and begin to rely on blood glucose. Consuming carbohydrate during a long ride allows you to restock this glucose supply which, in turn, replenishes your energy.

(Just then, Ellen's chief rival, Donna, rides by. Ellen's heart sinks—she didn't think Donna was so close behind. Donna notices Ellen's surprise and slows just long enough to let a comment to a riding partner be overheard: "C'mon, let's get to the finish and pick up that patch." Ellen gets back on her bike and gives chase. And as she begins those last 25 miles, she reaches into her jersey pocket for more food and takes a long swig of the sports drink in her water bottle.)

Fluid-and-energy-replacement drinks have various names (such as Exceed, Hydra Fuel, Gatorade, Body Fuel 450) and generally contain 5 to 8 percent carbohydrate. They're important because they empty from the stomach faster than solid food and, thus, can be turned to energy quicker.

It's best to drink in small, frequent doses. Start drinking 15 minutes into any long ride, and take a few gulps every 10 to 15 minutes. This gives your system time to absorb the fluid, whether it's a sports drink or plain water. In general, continue to drink at least one bottle of fluid per hour.

Nibble frequently, too. Good, portable, high-carbo choices include bananas, bagels, muffins, low-fat cookies (such as oatmeal), fig bars, fruit, graham crackers, rice cakes and gorp (a homemade mix of cereal, raisins, dates, chocolate chips, etc.). Most commercial high-energy bars are good choices, too. (Check their labels to determine carbohydrate and fat content.) Another option is a liquid food such as Ultra Energy. This product contains three to five times as much carbohydrate and calories as most conventional sports drinks. Not everyone can stomach such mixtures, however, and it is expensive. One water bottle's worth of Ultra Energy costs $5.50. Never use a new food or drink during an important ride before trying it in training.

Time Your Snacking for Best Results

For best results, start eating about 30 minutes into a long ride, and eat something at least every half hour afterward. The best time is on the flats or during a gradual descent, where trying to chew and swallow won't interfere with breathing. When riding with a group, wait until you're at the back of the pack to eat. Then a swerve caused by fooling with food won't result in a crash.

Don't succumb to cravings for high-fat foods such as chips, cakes, nuts, meats and cheeses. They're less efficient as fuel and take longer to digest, thus creating competition between your stomach and muscles for valuable oxygen-rich blood. In the end your muscles will win, but your stomach won't take the loss well. Nausea and vomiting may result.

(Before long, Ellen catches the group her rival is in. It appears Donna was putting on a good show at the rest stop because she isn't looking too fresh now. In fact, she's struggling to keep pace and weaving slightly. "What's the matter," Ellen asks, pulling alongside. "I don't know," Donna says with considerably less cockiness than before. "I feel weak, shaky. I think I'm going to have to stop." Later, it's learned that Donna had pedaled past the last three rest stops and hadn't eaten anything in three hours.)

If you don't eat and drink properly during a long ride, you'll not only deplete your muscle glycogen but also your blood glucose. To scientists, the resulting condition is known as hypoglycemia. Among cyclists, it's called the bonk. Since the central nervous system is fueled by blood glucose, exhausting these important stores can have serious consequences. Your body may react with dizziness, nausea, confusion and, sometimes, fainting.

Once again, carbohydrate is the answer. It goes directly into energy use, thus staving off the bonk. A recent study found that cyclists exercising at 70 percent intensity could ride an extra hour when carbohydrate was consumed. In fact, on any ride longer than three hours, the food and fluid you consume are as important as what you eat beforehand. One bout with the bonk will teach you the importance of that.

17 THE BONK

It's midday. Until a few moments ago, you were cruising along, feeling tip-top. Now routine tasks seem a little irksome. You go to downshift, only to discover that you're already in your lowest gear. You struggle toward the top, where your partner is standing beside his bike waiting for you to catch up. How come he looks so happy when all you can think about is heading home, preferably by car?

So, what's going on? A few minutes ago you felt terrific, but suddenly you're weak, irritable and wishing you didn't have to pedal another stroke. Why?

Simply put, you've bonked—you've met the bane of long-distance cycling.

The word "bonk" is traditional, and the condition feels just like the name sounds. It's used to describe the symptoms that occur when you deplete essential carbohydrate stores in your body as a result of sustained cycling. Once you experience it, you won't want it to happen again. This chapter will help you make sure it doesn't.

Your Fuel System

As you ride, most of the fuel being oxidized or burned is consumed by your active muscles. Both fat and carbohydrate can be utilized for this process. Fat, stored in fatty tissue, is reduced to free fatty acids and transported by the blood to the working muscles. In contrast, carbohydrate is stored within the muscles as glycogen, which is a long polymer composed of many glucose molecules. During exercise, individual molecules are removed from the polymer and used as energy.

Your vital organs *also* require a continuous supply of fuel, however. Whether at rest or during exercise, your brain and nervous system, for instance, depend upon blood glucose. The reason for this dependence is that the cells of your nervous system don't store glycogen and can't use fat. Thus, to meet energy requirements, blood glucose levels must be tightly regulated and maintained. This job is largely done by the liver, which contains large stores of glycogen that can be converted to glucose.

With the muscles and organs vying for glucose, extended exertion can drain the liver. When blood glucose levels become too low to meet the fuel requirements of your central nervous system, you begin feeling disoriented, tired, irritated and generally miserable. In a word, you bonk.

Even after this happens, though, you can save the ride. Despite how low blood glucose levels fall as a result of liver glycogen depletion, they can be replenished by eating or drinking something rich in carbohydrate. This is quickly digested into simple sugars that enter the bloodstream and are transported to the liver, muscles and other organs.

Even better, you can avoid bonking at all. By periodically eating or drinking small amounts of carbohydrate while riding, your stomach will be able to continuously add glucose to the blood. This will greatly reduce the drain on your liver's valuable glycogen stores. The trick is to begin eating or drinking about 15 minutes into a long ride and continue to do so every 10 to 15 minutes thereafter.

This isn't necessary on short rides, but the definition of "short" and "long" depends on your fitness. For novices, an hour-long ride is very long. For veteran endurance riders, two hours might be short. A good preventive measure in any case is to never leave home without your favorite energy food and/or drink—just in case.

Hitting the Wall

The terms "bonk" and "hitting the wall" are often used interchangeably, but there is a difference. Both are caused by fuel depletion. Unlike bonking, however, which is caused by the depletion of liver glycogen, hitting the wall stems from the depletion of muscle glycogen. Bonking is avoidable and curable. Hitting the wall can be delayed by ingesting carbohydrate, but once it happens, that's it—you're finished for the day.

The condition is so devastating because as the rate of fuel consumption rises in response to intensifying exercise, the muscles turn to their most readily available fuel—muscle glycogen. In fact, it's the only fuel that can support exercise at levels greater than 70 to 80 percent of VO_2 max. (Another reason muscle glycogen is so important is that it provides an essential intermediate product that's required to burn fat.) When you run out of muscle glycogen you're only able to exercise at very moderate intensity.

As with beating the bonk, the key to avoiding the wall is maintaining a steady intake of carbohydrate. Another trick is to avoid wasting the muscle glycogen you have. For instance, each time you jam a hill, your body switches to anaerobic metabolism to meet the extra energy demands. This process uses glycogen much less efficiently than aerobic metabolism. Therefore, on long rides, avoid blasting up climbs, always accelerate smoothly and resist all temptations to ride harder than usual.

Carbo Is Key

To avoid these dreadful conditions, eat and drink carbohydrate-rich products. Energy replacement drinks (available at most bike shops) are popular because they're effective. Typically, the powders consist of polymers or starches that mix with water to form 5 to 10 percent glucose solutions. Experiment with several brands until you find one that tastes good and agrees with your system.

Likewise, there are numerous energy supplement bars on the market that are excellent solid sources of carbohydrate. There are also many common, less-expensive alternatives, including fig bars, bagels, bananas, dried fruit and granola bars. As with energy drinks, experiment with different solid foods. Most long-distance riders settle on a combination of solid and liquid supplements to provide variety as well as energy replacement.

Whatever you select, remember to use it. You'd be amazed at how many experienced riders bonk or hit the wall with food still in their pockets. By sipping and nibbling every 10 to 15 minutes, you'll be able to avoid the bonk. And when the ride is over, you may even have energy left to clean the garage.

18 FAT AS FUEL

Attention, long-distance riders: Fat is your friend, despite the dire warnings you've read and heard so often. So enjoy your cookies, cake and mocha almond fudge ice cream. After all, you'll burn it.

Okay, maybe that's a slight exaggeration. But the theory is sound. Unknown to many, fat is the body's primary fuel when riding below about 80 percent of capacity. You can go all day on the stuff. Problem is that most of us store more than enough of this gelatinous substance without even trying. The result is well known and potentially embarrassing when wrapped in Lycra.

So while you probably don't need to eat more fat, you can improve your ability to burn it, and this can improve endurance and give you more energy in the final portion of a long ride. Just ask Andy Hampsten, who has twice finished in the top ten of the three-week-long Tour de France. He attributes much of this success to tuning what he calls his "fat engine."

"You need to learn how to burn fat, not just carbohydrate," he explains. "I've had a lot of problems using just carbohydrate. The first few years in Europe I did that. Now I have much more endurance."

A Second Wind

Exercise physiologists have long preached the benefits of a high-carbohydrate, low-fat diet, and justifiably so. Carbohydrate is the primary fuel for intense muscle contraction, and its energy is released as much as three times as fast as that from fat. But its supply is limited. Carbohydrate stores are typically exhausted during the second hour of fairly intense exercise. In comparison, there is theoretically enough fat for several days of low-intensity activity.

The challenge for endurance cyclists is to save the all-important carbohydrate stores for the most intense part of a ride. For Hampsten, this means the final two hours of a six- or eight-hour race.

"When I was competing more in the U.S., I was good just for short, high-intensity efforts," he says. "Now I seem like this incredible diesel. In Europe the races are longer, and I need a larger amount to draw on.

"I think of fat as my 80 percent engine. You can't sprint on it, but it saves glycogen [stored carbohydrate] for later. You've heard of a second wind. That's exactly what this is."

You're probably thinking that this is fine for someone such as Hampsten, who carries a mere 5 to 6 percent body fat on his frame most of the year. He can afford to tinker with his fat engine. But what about the rest of us? Fortunately, the key lies in changing the mechanism, not the intake. Physiologists note that with training, athletes can exercise at a higher percentage of max using fat as energy. For example, an untrained person uses mostly fat up to about 50 percent of max, then switches to carbohydrate. But with proper training, fat can supply the gas up to 80 percent of max.

Hampsten's guru for this regimen is Massimo Testa, an Italian doctor who serves as physician for the Motorola pro team. "Andy had a very strict diet and was stressed out about fat," says Testa. "He ate a lot of complex carbohydrate—cereals and vegetables. That's fine for short races—

a couple hours at most. But when the races are longer, if you can't use fat you'll be in trouble."

The Ironies of Low-Carbo Training

So how is it done? Hampsten uses two methods. Both emphasize long, easy rides without a lot of carbohydrate. This forces the body to tap its fat supply. And with time, you get better at using it.

Assuming Sunday included a long, strenuous ride that depleted your muscle glycogen, Testa recommends the following training for Monday: "For breakfast eat meat, eggs and orange juice, but don't take on a big carbohydrate load such as cereal or fruit. After such a meal you won't be able to ride at a high intensity and your efficiency will suffer 15 to 20 percent. Go for a very easy, long ride of about three hours, which is best for the utilization of fat."

Another method Hampsten uses was suggested by Charlie Hanson, his training partner and a former racer. Once per week he goes on a morning ride but doesn't begin eating until after one hour. "It can be hard psychologically because I love breakfast," says Hampsten. "But within an hour I've burned all my glycogen. And once I've turned on the fat-burning engine, it seems to stay on."

Testa is emphatic about the fact that "people should know I don't want them to eat more fat. For a cyclist the daily intake should be 20 to 25 percent of total calories, and that's pretty low." Even Hampsten says he hasn't increased consumption of dietary fats. "I try to limit my fat, but at the same time I don't deprive my body of it," he says. "Some people can be fanatical about it. I don't eat fried food or pastries, and I've cut dairy products. But I love olive oil and butter."

Overall, Hampsten insists that this isn't just a program for racers. "It's important for anyone who doesn't want to be at the whim of their glycogen level. Why should you have to worry that you'll bonk if you run out of food and it's more than an hour to the next store?

"And besides, it's fun. At the end of a long ride when you should be shattered, you'll feel good."

Part Five

BIKE CARE

19 PRE-EVENT CHECKUP

There's an old maxim in bicycle racing that says, "To win, you have to finish." Fact is, this bit of wisdom applies to all cycling events, from informal group rides to centuries and beyond. You may be in the best possible condition, but it won't matter if your bike breaks down.

To make sure yours doesn't, here's a detailed inspection procedure. Do this at least two days before a major event, then if you find a problem you'll have time to fix it and test the repair with one more ride. If you don't have the necessary tools or mechanical know-how, arrange for quick service at a local bike shop. (For illustrated, do-it-yourself procedures, see another book in this series: *Bicycling Magazine's Basic Maintenance and Repair*.)

Tools to Have on Hand

You'll need 4-, 5- and 6-mm allen wrenches, 8-, 9-, 10- and 15-mm open-end wrenches, a socket wrench for the crankarms, screwdrivers, a spoke wrench, grease and spray lube. A repair stand is helpful but not essential. If bearing adjustments are required, you may need cone wrenches, a freewheel remover, headset wrenches, a 12-inch adjustable wrench, large locking pliers, a crankarm extractor and a bottom bracket wrench set. (Some shops may lend these tools.)

Drivetrain

Begin your once-over with the drivetrain.

Bottom bracket bearings. Shift to the small chainring and lift the chain onto the bottom bracket with your finger. Spin the crank. It should turn freely. Push and pull the crankarms to check for bearing play. If there is any roughness or looseness, use a lockring spanner and pin tool to adjust the bearings. (On most cranksets you can do this without removing the crankarms.) Even if the bottom bracket feels okay, try tightening the lockring to make sure it's snug.

Crankarm bolts. Unscrew the crankarm dustcaps and tighten the mounting bolts or nuts with a socket wrench. Grease the threads and reinstall the caps.

Chainring bolts. Tighten these with a 5-mm allen wrench. (You may need to hold the nuts on the back of the rings with your finger, a chainring bolt tool or a screwdriver.)

Pedals. Tighten each one to the crankarm with a 15-mm wrench.

Toe clips and straps. Check clips for cracks and straps for grooves that could cause slipping. Replace if necessary. Tighten the mounting hardware with a screwdriver and wrench.

Chain. Backpedal with the chain on the smallest freewheel cog. If there are any stiff links, you'll see them clunk through the rear derailleur pulleys. To remedy this, grasp the chain on either side of the stiff link and work it until it loosens. If there are more than two stiff links, replace the chain.

Measure the chain with a ruler. Start on the center of any pin and look at the 12-inch mark. If that pin is ⅛ inch or more past the mark, the chain has stretched and should be replaced.

Apply spray lube and go for a short ride. Pedal hard in each gear to test for skipping. This commonly occurs after replacing the chain and indicates worn teeth on the freewheel. To correct this, replace the offending cog(s) or the entire cluster, using the removal tool made for your brand.

Gear cables. Check at the levers, under the bottom bracket and near the derailleur anchor bolts for rusting and fraying. Replace if necessary. If shifting is sluggish, grease the cables where they pass through the housing.

Rear derailleur. Shift to make sure there is no hesitation when going to the largest or smallest cog. If shifting is sluggish or if the chain derails, adjust the limit screws. (These are sometimes marked "L" for low gear and "H" for high gear.)

To fine-tune an index ("click shift") system, use the adjustment barrel located where the cable enters the derailleur. Turning the barrel counterclockwise quickens shifting to larger cogs, while turning it clockwise improves shifting to smaller ones. Adjust it a half turn at a time, then check performance.

Front derailleur. Shift forcefully, making sure the chain doesn't fall off and the cage doesn't hit the crankarm. If either happens, adjust the limit screws.

Derailleur bolts. Gently tighten the bolts that secure the derailleurs, pulleys, front derailleur cage and cables.

Wheels

Here, too, preventive maintenance is de rigueur.

Hub bearings. Remove both wheels. Grasp the axle locknuts and try unscrewing them with your fingers. If they loosen, use cone wrenches to tighten them against the cones. (On rear wheels this requires removing the freewheel.) Turn the axle to check for resistance. Loosen the cone adjustment if necessary. Check bearing play by trying to move the axle up and down. A little play is permissible if it disappears when the wheel is clamped in the frame. Once the wheels are installed, recheck the play by trying to move the rim laterally. If there is movement, remove the wheel and tighten the cone adjustment.

Spokes. Wiggle each one, and use a spoke wrench to tighten any that are loose. True both wheels as necessary.

Tires. They should have ample tread (no bare patches) and no large cuts. Also, check the sidewalls for cracks or bulges. If problems exist, replace the tires. Another test is to inflate the tires and spin them to make sure there are no flat or high spots. If the tires aren't round, let the air out and reinflate. If the problem persists, buy new tires.

Brakes

Ensure your stopping power.

Mounting bolts. Gently tighten the nuts located behind the fork crown and in front of the rear brake bridge. Use a 5-mm allen wrench or a 10-mm open-end wrench. Tighten cantilever brakes with a 5- or 6-mm allen wrench.

Lubrication. Spray some lube on the pivots and brake springs. (Don't get any on the brake pads or tires.)

Pads. If they've worn past their grooves, replace them. Be sure they don't touch the tire or go under the rim when the brakes are applied. Tighten their mounting nuts or bolts.

Cables. Inspect these for fraying inside the levers. Check for resistance that might indicate a bad cable. Lubricate or replace as necessary.

Front End

You'll also want to know what to look—and listen— for in your bike's front end.

Headset bearings. Check these by turning the handlebar with the front wheel off the ground. If the fork turns roughly, loosen the top nut and the adjustable cone underneath. Then tighten the nut and cone against each other with a pair of headset wrenches, or one headset wrench and a 12-inch adjustable wrench.

With both wheels on the ground, rock the bike back and forth with the front brake applied. A clunking noise indicates bearing play. Another way to check for this is to lift the front wheel several inches off the ground and drop it, listening for a rattling noise. Tighten the bearing adjustment if necessary.

Even if your headset passes these tests, make sure the top nut and cone are tight against each other.

Handlebar and stem. Check for stem tightness by lightly turning the handlebar with the front wheel between your knees. Press down on the ends of the bar to see if it rotates. Use a 5- or 6-mm allen wrench to tighten the stem expander bolt or the handlebar binder bolt, as necessary.

Levers. Check the tightness of brake and mountain bike shift levers by trying to twist them on the handlebar. To tighten drop bar brake levers, use a 4- or 5-mm allen wrench or an 8-mm socket inside the lever. Mountain bike controls are tightened with a 4-, 5- or 6-mm allen wrench or an 8-mm open-end wrench.

Seat

Stabilize your seat, too.

Saddle and seatpost. Tighten the seat clamp (under the saddle) with a 13-mm open-end wrench or a 6-mm allen wrench. Try twisting the saddle and seatpost in the frame. If it turns, tighten the seatpost binder bolt with a 5-mm allen wrench. On mountain bikes, tighten the quick-release lever.

Accessories

Don't overlook other important details.

Water bottle cage. Inspect it for cracks and replace if necessary. Gently tighten the mounting bolts.

Tire repair kit. Examine your spare tube and repair kit. Make sure the glue hasn't dried. Include a piece of sail cloth or denim. This can be temporarily placed inside the tire to "boot" large slits. Inflate a tire to check the operation of your frame pump.

EMERGENCY REPAIR KIT

We've heard of a bike mechanic who once rode across the country with only a pair of Vise-Grips in his tool kit. Few riders have the skill to make do with such minimal survival gear, so this chapter presents two lists of items to help deal with on-road breakdowns.

As a long-distance rider piling up big miles in training and events, someday you're bound to encounter a mechanical problem when you are far from help. By carrying the tools to do the repair, you can be on your way again in a few minutes, saving the ride. This is particularly important in a big event you've trained hard to prepare for, particularly those such as brevets or endurance time trials that have time limits. It's also part of being a responsible rider. By being self-sufficient, friends and family won't need to worry about your becoming stranded.

The Mini-Kit: Don't Leave Home without It

You should carry a primary tool kit on any ride that takes you farther than you'd care to return from on foot. In other words, consider this kit an essential bicycle component. The following items are meant to supplement the basic tools you should have in your home shop. Emphasis is on efficiency, low weight and minimal bulk. There are no extraneous items.

Before buying individual tools, visit a bike shop to see all-in-one tool kits designed for cyclists. These are compact, relatively light, and some are cunningly designed to include several unexpected tools. As this book was going to press, numerous such kits were coming onto the market.

Frame pump. It should fit snugly along the seat tube or the top tube (if the frame has a head tube pump peg). Clamp-on pump brackets are fine, too. Make sure the pump head fits the valves on your tubes. And check out the new mini-pumps, which are about one-third the size of a conventional model, making them lighter and easy to carry in a pack or even a jersey pocket. They work well, although considerably more strokes are required to inflate a tire.

Spare tube. Buy the correct size and valve. Dust it with talcum powder and wrap it in a plastic bag. Then wrap the bag with nylon-reinforced strapping tape to protect the tube from chafing. A piece of this tape can be used for an emergency tire boot.

Patch kit. Include a small tube of glue, four patches of various sizes and a tire boot (1 × 1-inch piece of old tire casing). The boot is necessary to save a severely cut tire, a problem that's more common since the advent of high-pressure clinchers with thin casings. Wrap the patch kit in masking tape to hold it together.

Tire levers. It's nearly impossible to remove a high-pressure clincher without these. Save some weight by choosing plastic instead of steel or aluminum. Although tire levers are normally sold in sets of three, you can always get by if you carry just two.

Spoke wrench. Pack the correct size for your spoke nipples—Japanese, European or DT.

Allen keys. Carry one for each hex bolt size on the bike. This means 4, 5, 6 and sometimes 7 millimeters.

Small adjustable wrench. A four-incher will fit nearly all the small nuts and bolts that might require adjustment in mid-journey.

Small folding knife. You need a single, 1¾-inch blade for cutting strapping tape, loose handlebar tape and tire boots.

Small screwdriver(s). A ⅛-inch blade and/or small Phillips screwdriver is necessary for derailleur adjustment screws and other small fittings, such as the computer mount.

Odds and ends. These are items that may be useful in a pinch: a presta-to-Schrader valve adapter (in case your pump breaks), spare toe clip bolts, change for the telephone, food money, a spare house key and an ID card. The spare change is for calling home when all else fails. The food money gives you the freedom to extend a 60-mile ride to 100 without bonking. Change and such can usually be stowed in a 35-mm film canister, but remember to restock it after use.

Saddle pouch. Buy a nifty under-the-seat bag to carry all this. If you own more than one bike, the bag can easily be transferred. If tire sizes are different, be sure to put in the correct spare tube.

The Maxi-Kit: Beyond the Basics

On multiday excursions, these items should be added to the basic kit. Unfortunately, you can't find a pro bike shop in every town. The things in this kit will help get you back on the road after encountering even major mechanical problems.

Folding tire and extra tube. Those of you who have asked for a 700C tire or presta-valve tube at the hardware store in Podunk, USA, will appreciate the need to carry these items on an extended tour. Folding tires with Kevlar beads are available in virtually all sizes, including mountain bike dimensions.

Freewheel remover and Pocket Vise. Carry the appropriate remover for your freewheel or Shimano Hyperglide lockring, and a Pocket Vise to hold the tool as you apply torque with your handlebar stem or a metal signpost. Those with a Shimano Freehub will have to carry a Cassette Cracker or two chainwhips in order to remove the cogs. Freewheel removal is necessary for spoke replacement on the right side of the hub.

Spare spokes. Carry 9 spokes (10 if you have a 40-spoke rear wheel) to replace the ones that get mangled if the chain shifts into them. Make sure they are the right size. Some riders keep spare spokes inside the frame pump. Another good idea is to tape them to the bike's left chainstay.

Spare cables. Properly maintained cables shouldn't break, but when they do, nothing will work in their place. Carry a rear brake cable and a rear derailleur cable (with the unneeded head removed if you buy the universal type). If a front cable breaks, install the replacement and coil the excess until you can trim it.

Adjustable cup tools. Park makes a lightweight universal pin tool and lockring tool. These are indispensable for adjusting a loose bottom bracket that would otherwise grind the crank innards into useless pulp if you continue pedaling.

Adjustable wrench. The six-inch size is handy for removing pedals and straightening chainrings.

Lubricants. Take a small tube of grease for sticky cables, and a small bottle of chain lube. Make sure the caps are tight, then wrap each in a rag and put them in zip-close plastic bags to prevent leakage.

Pliers. A small pair of channel-locks will do what the other tools won't.

Hand cleaner. For removing dirt and grease after a repair, carry a tube of waterless hand cleaner and some paper towels in a plastic bag to keep them dry.

CREDITS

The information in this book was drawn from these and other articles in *Bicycling* magazine.

"Paris-Brest-Paris: The King of Long-Distance Events" Ed Pavelka, "Time Waits for No One," December 1991.

"Become a Part of Cycling History" Bill Strickland, "You're History!" April 1992.

"Solutions to Saddle Sores" Steve Johnson, Ph.D., "Saddle Sores," October/November 1989.

"Hand Positions" Geoff Drake, "Hand Positions," August 1991.

"Long-Distance Comfort" Connie Carpenter Phinney, "Long-Distance Comfort," August 1988.

"22 Tips for Stronger Climbing" Ed Pavelka, "Climbing Clinic," April 1992.

"A Training Guide for Century Rides" Scott Martin, "Century Ride Training Guide," August 1988.

"Nine Days to Glory" Nelson Pena, "9 Days to Glory," September/October 1990.

"The Double Century" Chris Kostman, "The Double Century," April 1989.

"How to Guarantee a Great Ride" Nelson Pena, "Satisfaction Guaranteed," September/October 1991.

"Slump Busting" Scott Martin, "Slump Busters," August 1991.

"The Freshness Factor" Geoff Drake, "The Freshness Factor," November 1991.

"Beating Fatigue" Nelson Pena, "Beating Fatigue," July 1990.

"How to Ride through Winter" Fred Matheny, "How to Ride through Winter," December 1988.

"Getting Stronger, Cycling Longer" Fred Matheny, "Enter the Iron Age," December 1989.

"Eating for Endurance" Ellen Coleman, R.D., "Eating for Endurance," May 1989.

"The Bonk" Steve Johnson, Ph.D., "Bonk," September 1989.

"Fat as Fuel" Geoff Drake, "Fat as Fuel," December 1991.

"Pre-Event Checkup" Jim Langley, "Pre-Event Checkup," July 1989.

"Emergency Repair Kit" Don Cuerdon, "Emergency Repair Kit," April 1987.

Photographs

Pages 26–31: John Hamel
Page 71: Sally Shenk Ullman

Illustrations

Page 3: Map by Patti Rutman
Pages 91–94: Scott MacNeil